"*A New Kind of Big* is a timely, provocative, and compelling that highlights how kingdom-minded churches are measuring their impact, not just by the number of people in the sanctuary but by the transformational effect they are having on their communities. Chip has done a wonderful job of connecting his story with God's bigger story of transformation in Atlanta and in cities around the nation. It is a "must-read" for those who are thinking about community transformation."

—Eric Swanson, coauthor of *The Externally Focused Quest* and *To Transform a City*

"In *A New Kind of Big*, Chip tells the story of our journey to bring the hand into Perimeter's DNA. And it's the hand joined with the head and heart that has introduced us to a much healthier ministry—one of increasing influence."

—from the foreword by Randy Pope, pastor of Perimeter Church

"What a wonderful book! Most Christians would like to see their church make an impact on the community and the world but are overwhelmed with the task. This book is the remedy. It's practical, honest, clear, and 'doable.' But it's more than that. *A New Kind of Big* is exciting! It reminds us of what church is about, when sometimes we forget. Read this book! It could change the world . . . and your life!"

—Steve Brown, professor, Reformed Seminary, Orlando, FL; president and teacher on the syndicated radio program *Key Life*

"Helping churches expand their spiritual vision and discover new ways to connect with their communities is a path Chip Sweney knows well. Jesus didn't call us to live on a church island. He called us to 'Go.' Thankfully, *A New Kind of Big* shows us how. I highly recommend it."

—Robert Lewis, pastor-at-large, Fellowship Bible Church; author, *The Church of Irresistible Influence*

"A key part of our national ministry is to lift up significant practical and impactful resources that can help men and women in cities/communities across America and the world serve together for sustained evangelism and discipleship. This book by Chip is right on the mark. I recommend this book to all the tens of thousands of men and women across America who seek to be encouraged and equipped in this worthwhile ministry of reaching our communities and cities collaboratively with the good news of Jesus Christ proclaimed in word and practiced in deeds!"

—Jarvis Ward, National Facilitator City/Community Ministries, Mission America Coalition

"No matter how large a church is, it will never be large enough to meet the needs of our communities. We need to partner together in order to accomplish the Great Commission. Chip Sweney masterfully displays biblical principles in 3-D. After reading this book, I'm convinced we all need to become *A New Kind of Big*. This is a must-read."

—Tito Ruiz, pastor of En Español Ministries, The Bridge Church Atlanta

A NEW KIND OF
BIG

HOW CHURCHES OF ANY SIZE CAN PARTNER TO TRANSFORM COMMUNITIES

CHIP SWENEY

WITH KITTI MURRAY

BakerBooks
a division of Baker Publishing Group
Grand Rapids, Michigan

Published by Baker Books
a division of Baker Publishing Group
P.O. Box 6287, Grand Rapids, MI 49516-6287
www.bakerbooks.com

Printed in the United States of America

Library of Congress Cataloging-in-Publication Data

Sweney, Chip, 1964–
    A new kind of big : how churches of any size can partner to transform communities / Chip Sweney with Kitti Murray.
       p.   cm.
    Includes bibliographical references.
    ISBN 978-0-8010-1369-0 (pbk.)
    1. Communities—Religious aspects—Christianity. 2. Church work. 3. Big churches. 4. Small churches. 5. Church management. I. Murray, Kitti. II. Title.
BV625.S895 2011
253—dc22
                                                                2010027418

10   11   12   13   14   15   16   7   6   5   4   3   2   1

To Leigh Ann Sweney,
my wife,
and Caroline and Jack Sweney,
our children.
You have encouraged me, supported me, and motivated me
to go for it in life.
I love you more than you can imagine!

Contents

Acknowledgments

- My wife, Leigh Ann, did not know what she was getting into when we got married and both entered the business world. Eighteen months later I was in full-time ministry. I could never have done what I am doing in ministry without her support and her sacrifice.
- Matt Brinkley, Bob Sweet, Bob Carter, and Carl Wilhelm have mentored me in the ministry and in life. My internship under Matt changed my life and resulted in the deepest of friendships. Regular time with these men over fifteen years has challenged me and helped me grow.
- My team at Perimeter over the last eight years has been an integral part in creating this story. Thanks to Drue Warner, Jackie Dieter, Harvey Anderson, Carl Wilhelm, Tricia Stradley, Debra Potter, and Heidi Hooper.
- Unite! leadership and I are creating this story together, and these relationships are what drive the movement.
- Dan Case and Bill Wood, good friends and fellow staff members at Perimeter, continually encouraged me to write this book and would not let it go or let me give up.
- Bryan White and I are the best of friends, and he is my "twin" brother even though we have different skin colors! It has been an incredible ride since we launched Unite!

- Thank you to the people of Perimeter Church. This story is about what God has done in and through you to make kingdom impact in Atlanta and beyond. Thank you for your steps of faith!
- Randy Pope, founder of and lead teacher at Perimeter, has inspired me through his vision and leadership and released me to go for it in Atlanta.
- Eric Swanson, Andy Rittenhouse, Ray Williams, and Eric Marsh have coached, encouraged, and equipped me in getting our people out into the community, working together with others for kingdom impact.
- Tim Cummins, a great friend, who has connected us to amazing opportunities to live out the head, heart, and hand in apartment complexes.
- Tom Lutz was so gifted as our consultant and facilitator as we were dreaming about adding "the hand" and as he guided the Mercy Ministry Task Force. He kept great notes of all those early discussions, which have contributed to this book.
- Kitti Murray is an amazing writer and turned my words into "music."

Foreword

For nearly four decades I've watched the church search for its identity. This model versus that model, modern versus postmodern, and of course, church growth at all costs. Over the years I've become increasingly convinced that *healthy* is a word desperately needed to describe church.

For many years I've carried a reminder in my briefcase. It features requirements necessary for a church to be healthy. Chip's book, *A New Kind of Big*, expounds brilliantly on two of them:

- the church must be committed to "influence" rather than "success"
- to be a church of influence, the church must have a strong head, heart, and hand

In her early years, Perimeter Church had been deemed a successful church by most. We had a strong head (theological depth) and heart (missional zeal and passion for worship). But the hand (addressing community issues requiring mercy and justice) was conspicuously missing.

In *A New Kind of Big*, Chip tells the story of our journey to bring the hand into Perimeter's DNA. And it's the hand joined with the head and heart that has introduced us to a much healthier ministry—one of increasing influence.

And who better to tell the story than Chip. Without question, he, more than any other, has been responsible for leading us through these uncharted waters. Chip's heart for a broken community is as big as I've ever seen. And his insights and strategic thinking have been a unique blessing to me personally, to Perimeter Church, and to our community.

So now it's your turn. He's about to be a blessing to you!

Randy Pope
pastor, Perimeter Church

1

A New Kind of Big

Are You Ready to Dream Big Again?

You didn't sign up to make a small splash in the world. If you're in ministry, chances are you've got big things on your mind. Maybe you're not a mass-market kind of guy or a girl who longs to speak to thousands. But the reason you do what you do is—by definition— large. Maybe you're content to be a smooth stone skipping across the still surface of the lake. You're a light touch, but you want that touch to have a ripple effect before it dies. Or maybe you were born with a tsunami in your chest. Either way, when you heard the call to follow Jesus, you knew you were on to something big. And when that call led you to *lead*, well, your world got even bigger.

Somewhere along the way you joined a staff or volunteered at a church or ministry. You figured if you were to go anywhere at all, you would need to catch hold of some coattails. And the church seemed like the best place to grab hold. So you stepped up. You took a small, personal leap of faith with a big dream in your heart.

The dream was big because of God. The more you got to know him, the more compelled you were to make sure no one within your reach missed him. Loving. Kind. Merciful. Forgiving. All in bigger doses than you could imagine. You're still taking him in.

And the dream was big because of the need. From the beginning you found evidence of people living smaller lives than they were created to live. And because their lives didn't fit the original plan, they were suffering. You saw it in the faces of your neighbors' children after their parents divorced. You saw it in the outstretched hand of the homeless man who waits for a handout at a downtown intersection. You saw it on the news and in the missionaries' newsletters and in the newest movie about children and sex trafficking. The need was staggering. You're still taking that in too.

God is big. The need is big. And, slowly, you began to realize just how small you are.

How can one person, one church, one organization meet the needs of the world with the dynamic message of the living God? How can we, the church, have a big influence on the world? It's a question worth asking. It's a question the church has been trying to answer for centuries.

Big or Small?

The prevailing definition of "big" is pretty obvious. Big parking lots and buildings, big activity centers and sanctuaries. Massive media coverage, marketing, music production. Systems, strategies, and social networks. Compare our subculture to the world. Big means keeping step.

Or does it? Measure the dimensions of your impact this way and this way alone, and you will most likely end up empty—full of improvements but wondering where the kingdom value leaked out of your life's work. You've probably had those existential moments when you've questioned the relevance of big. Like a landscaper who develops a plan that requires hours and hours of upkeep, you don't have time to sit back and absorb the beauty. You know why you're doing it that way, but at times you forget.

But does that make "small" the way to go? Maybe you've viewed the church as a Walden's Pond, a place to retreat from the glitz and to trim your ideology down to its simple roots, a place to stay focused. Sure, small scale has its benefits, but that doesn't make the need any smaller. Sure, the relationships formed in a smaller setting are meaningful, but what about the masses? How many times has a small group soured because it failed to look outside its comfortable boundaries? And when a small church reaches out, how effective can it be without the resources of its mega brothers?

Or maybe you've yo-yoed between a love affair with the sheer power of the large and the sweet simplicity of the small. You aren't a consumer. You are consumed with a mission. You have a job to do, and you want to get it done. You really want to know which works best.

And maybe, just maybe, you've been addressing the wrong issue. Think about it. The problem with the church is not its size (or, rather, the size of its gatherings); the problem with the church is its reach. When you suspect that the church has minimal or even non-existent influence, *that's* what provokes your heart. Isn't it? That's what you really care about. That's why you started this journey in the first place.

Go back to how it all started. It began with something big. The God of the universe touched your life and longs to touch people—entire communities even—through you and others like you. You are down the line from those first disciples who "turned the world upside down" (Acts 17:6 ESV) in the first century. Yes, big is important but not for the reasons that can easily consume you if you are part of an institution or organization that keeps records, counts heads, or builds buildings. (No matter the size of your church, it's all too easy to trip over these things on your way to the "real" stuff.)

Big is important because God is bigger than his own creation, bigger than his church in all its expressions, bigger than his heaven. Huge.

And big is important because the need is big. The issues—like injustice and poverty and hunger—are bigger than any one person can address. Our cities and countries and continents are bigger than any one church can influence.

The Drama

This is a drama of epic proportions, and the big versus small debate hardly matters at all.

Here is the pivotal question: How in the world can churches—no one church is big enough—make a God-sized impact on a world with God-sized needs? Or preface that question with this one: If your church ceased to exist tomorrow, what impact would that have on the people living in a twelve-mile radius of your front door? What about the kindergartener at the elementary school five miles away who's in the free lunch program because Dad left and Mom can barely make ends meet even though she works fifty to sixty hours a week? What does your church have to offer *that* kindergartener? Are you making a difference? Is your church making a difference? Is making a difference possible? What if it could be done? What if someone tried and lived to tell the tale?

What if, indeed?

You are not the only one with a big dream in your heart. You know that. But did you know others are beginning to succeed in their pursuit of that dream? One church, Perimeter Church in Atlanta, united with over one hundred other churches in one city for this purpose alone. Each church laid aside its own agenda to serve a big God and meet a big need. And it worked. It's still working. Here's a wide-angle view of the combined firepower of these churches: On just one weekend in 2007, six thousand volunteers from over sixty churches gathered to work on 250 service projects inside the twelve-mile radius around Perimeter Church. Thirty welcome baskets were delivered to refugees, a dozen homes were repaired, a thousand Bibles were given away, 750 "encourage a teacher" gift bags were distributed. And that's not all. Volunteers orchestrated twenty block parties in low-income apartment communities and sixty-five neighborhood food drives that collected twenty-five-thousand pounds of food.

The drama is in the impossibility of the task. This book is the tale of how the people of Perimeter Church joined people from other churches to address an "impossibly" big need. The service projects mentioned above didn't just happen. They grew out of relationships between churches and the community. And those relationships were formed in response to huge issues such as poverty, education, family, and justice. These churches refused to limit their definition of big to buildings, gatherings, or parking lots. They shared a love for God and an ache to extend his hand to the world in significant ways.

This book is not an instruction manual; it is a story. It is not written from the pedestal but from the pit of need. It does not outline the small stuff; it proposes the big. And it is an open invitation to your own bigger story.

Maybe over the years your dream has become smaller. Who can blame you really? I mean, if you dream big and it doesn't work out, you're left with a broken heart. People give up on their dreams all the time, and it's understandable. The problem is, as beings created by a big God, we were meant for big things. So you can give up on your dreams, but it won't result in a fulfilling life. Sadly, if you choose this path, you will have settled, sold out.

This book is for people who are ready to think big again, ready to grapple with the ancient, fiery questions in the crucible of this drama. Because that's what your mission is about. The Christian task encompasses "the ends of the earth." In other words, while fully aware that you are small and your church is too, God has given you an assignment with an unlimited reach. He has had big in mind all along.

Think about It

At the end of each chapter, you will be given an opportunity to pause and process what you've just read. Because I honestly don't know what big will look like in your life or in the life of your church, the work to be done in this section is all yours. I encourage you to dig deep here, to be honest about "what is" and courageous about "what could be."

I also encourage you to answer these questions, if possible, in the company of other leaders in your church or ministry. They were written for people who not only want to think big but also want to put big into practice. The questions represent a progression that goes like this:

What is . . .

Where are you and your church right now? Are you currently addressing the issues presented in the chapter?

What could be . . .

I will ask you to look ahead several years, to dream about what might happen.

What will be . . .

What steps can you take right now? In each chapter, you will set a few simple goals that will help you and your church put things in motion.

What we did . . .

How did Perimeter Church do it? You won't do it the same way, but it may be helpful to read a brief summary of Perimeter Church's action steps.

To find out more information about what Perimeter is doing, go to www.anewkindofbig.com.

Picture This

Each chapter will also end with a metaphor—a picture of something tangible, something of unparalleled function or beauty (or both) that is ineffective if it stands alone, something that derives its highest value and splendor by blending with similar elements. The strands of a rope, the threads in a tapestry, the words in a sentence, the links in a chain . . . you get it. Here the material in each chapter is presented as a visual parable. So picture this.

In 1666, Sir Isaac Newton observed that, in all of art and nature, just three colors exist: red, yellow, and blue. All other colors are derived from these three. We know them as the primary colors, the three spokes in the color wheel. Simple. But what wonders are wrought when just three basic, pure, unadulterated colors collide!

Combine two—yellow and blue—to make green. US currency. Oz. The canopy of a rain forest. A gardener's thumb.

But it's much more complicated than that. Colors have things like values and saturations. They are either warm or cool. The study of colors is a veritable science. Did you know red can seem brighter against a black background and somewhat duller against a white background? In contrast with orange, red looks lifeless; in contrast with blue-green, it shines.[1]

The best dreams are in color, aren't they? To say something is colorful is to say it is the product of expert integration, of the amalgam of more than one hue. In other words, living color is only found when various elements are joined together. Again, colors are meant to mix. As you read on, you'll find that the dream that became Unite! was and is synergistic: the product of mixing. It has been the blending together of people, gifts, ideas, visions, and churches. As in a work of art, the mixture is what has given it depth and beauty.

> Why do two colors, put one next to the other, sing? Can one really explain this? No.
>
> Pablo Picasso

> Walk into the fields and look at the wildflowers. They don't fuss with their appearance—but have you ever seen color and design quite like it?
>
> Luke 12:27 Message

2

Turning Our Hearts Inside Out

First Steps toward Becoming a Church of Influence

Looking back, it was an abrupt awakening. In reality, it was the slow unfurling of a life-changing message in my heart. The really surprising part is the messengers by which it came.

It all began during seminary. While attending school in Chicago from 1993 to 1996, I served as a part-time staff member at Winnetka Bible Church. At Winnetka, I began to discover an untapped resource for ministry—an indefatigable group of people.

This lively group exists in every city, populates every church, and can penetrate every culture. They are unencumbered by the normal stresses of life, yet they are as embattled as the rest of us, if not more so. They may be bruised, but they are not bitter. And talk about easy to motivate! Because they typically lack cynicism, it takes very little exposure to the needs of others for them to spring into action. Just give them a few well-aimed nudges.

I'm talking about junior high kids. No, I don't know kids from another planet. And, yes, I know what they're really like. I'm also aware of the current research that reveals that the prefrontal cortex of a teenager's brain doesn't develop until around age eighteen.[1] That explains the deficiencies in their ability to plan, remember where their backpacks are, organize simple tasks, and control their wildly fluctuating moods. But I also know what I've observed. Young teenagers have tender hearts.

Some parents who had their children at a young age talk about "growing up with" their kids. Well, I "grew up" into missions with my junior high kids. It began at Winnetka, where the kids in my youth group and I began to live out the gospel in both word and deed. We learned firsthand about the needs of our cities together. We took action together. I'm still not sure who led the way.

At Winnetka, our eyes were opened to the complicated needs of the inner-city poor in Chicago. This wasn't an overseas mission trip experience for us; it was in our own backyard. The needs were impossible for us to ignore. Every couple of months we went as a group and spent time with children who were part of a ministry called Inner City Impact. These experiences brought the reality home that significant needs were not far from us.

After seminary I moved to Atlanta to become the junior high pastor at Perimeter Church, and the story at Winnetka repeated itself. While in this role from 1996 to 2002, I discovered similar needs in our city and a similar resource in our church: teenagers. At Perimeter, I observed kids making a difference on mission trips and realized that their talent for touching lives could become a lifestyle if they had an outlet nearby. I wanted to "get in the game" and decided to take them with me.

Once a month—instead of bowling, putt-putt, or some other form of entertainment—we did what we called Mission Mania. We went to a village for the mentally challenged to develop relationships, play games, and love them. While this was good, I was burdened to give students more opportunities to give themselves away in the community. Then I met a man named Tim Cummins, whose ministry, Whirlwind Missions, was mobilizing churches to serve in apartment complexes that were full of immigrants and refugees. We mobilized our students to do Bible clubs in these apartment complexes, where the parents often could not speak English. That grew into an after-school program. Momentum built, and members of our student ministry began serving in more complexes. Soon, adults were joining us to teach English and to tutor. A movement was beginning, but

The Power of Suggestion

Brian was a junior high student at Perimeter who helped out at a transitional village for homeless families. One summer we suggested—well, challenged, really—the students to give away something they owned to the children at the village. Brian was an avid hockey player and had a garage full of hockey sticks. It would have been easy for him to polish up an old stick and give it away. It would have been a powerful gesture—especially to the child who received it. But Brian did something more powerful: He gave away his newest, prized stick, the one he played with all the time. Little did he know he was setting an example for our entire church. Brian's gift paved the way for a culture shift among his peers. Giving became second nature to many of the kids, and their parents began to notice. Giving our prized possessions away—isn't that the truest picture to the world of the gospel in action?

most couldn't see it. Maybe that's because they didn't expect it to begin with middle school kids.

A Vision Is Born

While the junior high kids at Perimeter and I were learning all about missions together, our pastor, Randy Pope, was ignited by a similar flame. In 2001, he explained a simple paradigm of a healthy church:

head (theology) + heart (passion) + hand (external ministry)

Randy shared with the Perimeter staff that he felt the church was missing this last key ingredient, the hand. He confessed his regret that our church was not strategically caring for those with significant needs outside our own doors. As Perimeter neared the celebration of its twenty-fifth anniversary, he charged the leaders to devise a plan to engage with the community and serve its needs. Because of my experience connecting junior high kids with the community, this was a challenge I was uniquely prepared to hear. He called for the church to "become a church of influence and to turn itself inside out for the least and the lost." Change was in the wind.

Solomon, in his wisdom, advised, "It is good that you grasp the one and do not let the other slip from your hand" (Eccles. 7:18 HCS). For twenty-five years Perimeter had built its ministry on a solid foundation—solid enough to provide a launchpad for new work, solid enough to produce the godly leadership for it, solid enough to provide biblical guidance.

One reason community outreach at Perimeter has been so successful is that the initial vision of community transformation fell on fertile soil. The reflexes of its members tended toward obedience. Their heads and their hearts were mature enough to do the next thing: to extend their hands to the least and the lost.

As a leader and staff member at Perimeter, I was required to do more than promote programs; I was to share my life in discipleship relationships. We were all accountable to operate on this basic level, including Randy. Jesus did it. His disciples did it. And they passed the pattern along to the next generation.

When members of a church are engaged in life-on-life missional discipleship, the church is the healthiest it can be, the most holistic. It is a church where heads, hearts, and hands join together. For example, before Randy's vision eventually grew to become a fully staffed Community Outreach department, I was meeting regularly

Write It Down

Daniel Boorstin, author of *The Creators* (Vintage, 1993) and *The Discoverers* (Vintage, 1985), once said that the written word was the greatest technology man ever invented.[2]

Documentation is the difference between getting everything you need for the dinner party at the grocery store or making a second trip; putting the mower back together safely or almost losing a toe when you discover you forgot an essential step in the process; filling the prescription (if you are a pharmacist), bypassing the artery (if you are a cardiothoracic surgeon), navigating the landing (if you are a pilot) correctly and saving lives or doing it incorrectly and endangering them.

So much hinges on the written word. Visions don't become plans unless things are written down.

Randy's initial vision to extend Perimeter's hands to the world, to become a church of influence, and to turn our hearts inside out for the least and the lost became a short manuscript. And that's where we started. One simple reason we moved was because the vision was documented.

for discipleship with a group of junior high boys. At the same time, I was prompted by the Spirit to lead in the area of ministry to the community. It just made sense—at this basic, cellular level—to involve my teenage guys in mission. We studied the Word together, we shared our lives, and we began meeting once a month to tutor children in need. All three elements in concert made the picture complete.

When discipleship is going on in a church, it's hard to compartmentalize its ministries. Missions becomes a function of relationships in response to God's call. Giving becomes a communal act born out of more than a sermon on tithing. Worship is a dance of interwoven lives in motion. Holiness is organic and real, something each person hammers out in the context of discussion and debate and the support of friends. And a movement—like the gathering firestorm of Unite!—can be as deep as it is wide.

To learn more about Perimeter's vision and life-on-life missional discipleship, read Randy's book *The Intentional Church*.[3]

Community Outreach

Randy's vision became an electric force throughout the church, but that's all it was at first. It was a force to be reckoned with but not yet a plan. In the chapters that follow, you will read more about the process we went through. In the beginning, Randy, the elders, and some key staff members began the process of thinking and praying together. Then they assigned a Mercy Ministry Task Force to gather information and make recommendations about the next decisions. These leaders also read Robert Lewis's book *The Church of Irresistible Influence* as they continued to pray and dream about the future.

The next step was to create an in-house entity—a Community Outreach department—to send our people out into the community. We wanted not only to bring healing to those who had been treated unjustly but also to end the practice of injustice. This meant working not only with individuals but also with organizations such as schools and government agencies. It proved to be a pivotal move.

By devoting staff and other resources to our city, we were following a powerful kingdom premise. In other words, the kingdom has priority over the local church. To advance the kingdom message into the world would cost us something not just individually but as a church. The decision to establish the Community Outreach department translated that cost into a very real budget and a very real staff.

This kingdom premise isn't limited to churches with large budgets. For smaller churches it may mean a key layperson who can chair a lay leadership team to implement a local mercy and justice ministry through the church. The key here is priority. Will the church give priority to the needs outside its doors? Will the church free up resources—people, money, programs—to focus on local ministry instead of devoting all of its capital to its own needs?

In 2002, I left my role as junior high pastor to become the director of this department. The Community Outreach department, which still exists today, is the primary means by which Perimeter sends its own people out into the community. Just as I had worked to engage our junior high kids in hands-on ministry to the least and the lost of our city, I was now faced with the task of engaging the rest of the church in the same kind of ministry.

The first thing we did in the summer of 2002 was to research the twelve-mile radius around our church to discover the needs and to find the groups already meeting those needs. We did more thorough research later, but for now it might help to know a little about what we did as a first step.[4] We hired two seminary students who performed the research on a very basic level. There were two stages in the process:

- First, the students compiled data from county websites to provide the demographics of the twelve-mile radius around our church. This wasn't very precise because the area includes portions of several counties.
- Second, they conducted interviews with select leaders, ministries, and organizations in the community. While even less scientific, this gave us a more human connection with the needs in the surrounding areas.

One major benefit of our initial research was that it helped us to find partners in the community. From the beginning we wanted to partner with those who were already engaged in ministry. We then began to deploy our people to get involved with those partners. It was gratifying work. It still is. But in the process, we discovered that the needs were bigger than our church could handle. Even with our big group of willing, mature volunteers, we couldn't tackle them alone.

In the beginning, the Community Outreach staff members were viewed as the "doers" of the ministry. The department's mandate, however, was to build strategic bridges with partners in the community and to provide opportunities for our people to serve. As vision casters and equippers, we had to learn how to work together with other departments in our church in order to get our people involved. As the director of Community Outreach, I had to lead the way. It wasn't easy at first, but I learned from others, like Rick Rusaw at Lifebridge Church in Longmont, Colorado. Each department at Lifebridge is required to build into its annual goals a plan to get people serving in the community. Such efforts help transfer the DNA of *doing* from the visionaries through the staff to the congregation.

These initial steps may seem like a painfully slow beginning. But this kind of thorough, thoughtful approach to ministry preparation provides a powerful start to a movement. Like the rich fuel gathering beneath a space shuttle on the launchpad at Cape Canaveral, the work of the task force readied us to move with lightning speed when the time came. The fueling process is forgotten in the drama of liftoff. When we finally began, we were a long way along the trajectory of our flight plan because of the decisions previously made by the task force.

Unite!

In 2003, Perimeter Church joined together with a network of other churches to create Unite!, a group of about 150 churches who do—together—what we set out to do in our twenty-fifth year: to transform our community by reaching the least and the lost. When Unite! launched and I was asked by the churches to be the director, I was still the Community Outreach director at Perimeter. I did this for several years and then transitioned leadership of Community Outreach to other Perimeter staff members. Although these two groups have a similar vision, they are not interchangeable. Community Outreach is an entity of the church, fully staffed and funded by Perimeter. Unite! is staffed and funded by local churches who "give away" staff time for the movement. As you read on, the details will become clearer, just as they did for us over time. To find out more information about Community Outreach at Perimeter as well as Unite!, go to www.anewkindofbig.com.

Within a few short years of the initial vision, the Community Outreach department at Perimeter and a movement of churches called Unite! had been birthed. Both were devoted to helping the church meet the needs of the community. Both were committed to the overall goal of community transformation. Both were focused not on the agenda of one local church but on the work of the kingdom in the city. But these things take time. It didn't happen overnight. In fact, before either Community Outreach or Unite! existed, the Mercy Ministry Task Force met for nine months to set the stage. In the beginning, the structure of the leadership wasn't clear. It wasn't a neat, perfectly linear, predictable process. There were lots of blanks to fill in before we were up and running. One of those blanks—one that would have stopped us in our tracks if we hadn't filled it—was money.

Because the challenge to turn our hearts inside out for the least and the lost was a pervasive part of our vision as a church, Perimeter made the commitment to fund the first steps. When we formed the Community Outreach department in 2002, we were given initial financial support via a ministry and campus development campaign. Over a three-year period, the staffing and program costs for Community Outreach were absorbed into the general budget, thanks to continued, strong church growth. Note that our church grew while we focused not.on our church but on the community around us.

The capital campaign to support Perimeter's Community Outreach department generated a lot of excitement in the church. We were not just raising money for new facilities; we were raising money to give ourselves away to the community and to the world. It was as if the desire to burst through the four walls of our church was primed and just about ready to explode. People just needed a vision and a way to give themselves to it.

Five years later, in 2007, as Perimeter continued to invest in the kingdom both locally and globally, we initiated a second capital campaign to raise funds above and beyond our general budget, this time exclusively for external ministry. The capital campaign allocated a large sum of money over a five-year time frame for "kingdom investments." Today, local or global partners can submit grant requests to Kingdom Investments for funding. The Kingdom Investments fund helped us take the next step toward partnering with other churches and ministries. Unlike the funds available in 2002, which were used primarily to build the internal infrastructure and staffing of outreach ministries, these funds are used solely for external initiatives.

The Community Outreach department is a part of Perimeter's staff and programming and is funded by our general budget. That means, like Brian's hockey sticks, these resources are ours to give away. We pour ourselves, our money, our time, and our planning into this department, only to pour them back into the community. In 2002, before we launched Community Outreach, about 11 percent of our overall general budget was allocated for missions, and almost all of this was global. Now, almost 23 percent of our general budget is for our ministries that reach beyond our four walls both locally and globally.

Randy had challenged us to turn our hearts inside out, to give ourselves, our possessions, and our church itself away. Clearly our people bought into the vision. They still do. They have turned not only their hearts inside out but also their pockets. Their regular support of Perimeter Church and Community Outreach provided the encouragement we needed to get things started and the resources to keep them going.

It's All in the DNA

We're only in chapter 2, and already we're talking about capital campaigns, full-time staff, and full-fledged departments. Your church may not have even considered these possibilities. You're thinking, *If that's what it takes to move people into the community with God's mercy and love, I'm sunk.*

Relax. It's not about staff and money. It's about people and resources. Think loaves and fishes. Think twelve dedicated, determined men (and not a single seminary education in the mix). Think small gatherings in catacombs and prison lunch-and-learn meetings.

The churches that joined with us and became Unite! are all different sizes. Some are wealthy; many are not. Some are mega; lots of them are mini. And remember, the beginning wave of community outreach hit our shore in the form of a small army of junior high kids. Believe me, it wasn't very sophisticated.

A spreading virus is never any different in its essence than each individual cell. The cell holds the precious DNA, the tiny map of its meaning, the recipe for its nature. It's an unfortunate metaphor, but it works. The needs of the world are big. The grace and mercy of God are bigger. All we're called to do is introduce the former to the latter. That's our DNA. And it doesn't matter how big *we* are to get the job done.

Think about It

What is . . .

What is your church doing currently to provide opportunities for the development of the head? The heart? The hand?

What ministries does your church provide for the spiritual formation of your people? Is what you are currently doing producing mature, equipped, and missional followers of Christ? If not, why not?

What could be . . .

It is five years down the road and your church is clearly successful in life-on-life discipleship. Mature, equipped, missional disciples are everywhere!

- What were the critical factors that led to success?
- What were the greatest obstacles to overcome?
- What were the early indicators that your efforts were heading in the right direction?

What will be . . .

What are several strategic steps you need to take to enhance or change your church's current spiritual formation process to one that can better develop mature, equipped, and missional followers of Christ? What are several action steps to take in the next six months?

What we did . . .

Perimeter is a big church with a big staff. But in one area, we have persistently kept things small. From the top down, we are committed to life-on-life discipleship. Our pastor does it, our staff members do it, our members do it. We don't just talk about it; we get in small groups and do it. And it is just as no-frills as it sounds. Here is a working definition from Randy Pope, our pastor:

> One way to define life-on-life missional discipleship is laboring in the lives of a few with the intention of imparting one's life, the gospel, and God's Word in such a way as to see them become mature and equipped followers of Christ, committed to doing the same in the lives of others.

Picture This

If you are going to grow living cells in a laboratory, you might want a PhD around to guide you. That's because it's delicate business. Complicated. After all, you're intruding on a natural process in an unnatural way.

First, no two cells are exactly the same, so expect some surprises. Second, for cells to multiply in a dish, they must be dislodged periodically from a dense culture and put into a more sparse culture. Then they grow in density and have to be dislodged and moved to a sparse environment again, and so on. This is called seeding. The student or professor who seeds cells in order to research them knows the cells must be watched vigilantly. Laziness or neglect may ruin the cells and sabotage the entire procedure. Some cells are adherent, meaning they are more difficult to dislodge. In that case, a process called trypsinization is required. Scientists have to baby the cells,

31

visiting the lab in early mornings and on weekends to keep the cycle moving along. It is a complex kind of hand-holding.[5]

Yet the cells themselves do the real work. And the DNA inside each cell determines the intricate pattern of life that unfolds.

In some ways, this is what those of us who lead in the body of Christ are here to do. We dislodge people from the dense population of church and move them to the sparsely populated (by Christians) culture of the world. We coach, offer encouragement, and sit back to let the DNA work. A farmer doesn't yell "Apple!" at his trees, does he? He just plants the seed, helps along the environment as much as he is able, and waits for the tiny pattern that shouts "apple" inside each seed to emerge on its own.

DNA. The imprint of reproducible life resides inside each of the redeemed. That's why it doesn't matter what size your church happens to be. Size is all about the God who planted himself inside you.

Physiologically, every cell in the human body is designed for every other cell. The whole purpose of each cell is to enable all the other cells to perform. The only cell that exists for itself is a cancer cell.

Tim Hansel, founder of Summit Expedition
and author of *Choosing Joy*

"All we have are five loaves of bread and two fish," they said. Jesus said, "Bring them here." Then he had the people sit on the grass. He took the five loaves and two fish, lifted his face to heaven in prayer, blessed, broke, and gave the bread to the disciples. The disciples then gave the food to the congregation. They all ate their fill. They gathered twelve baskets of leftovers.

Matthew 14:17–20 Message

The mystery in a nutshell is just this: Christ is in you.

Colossians 1:27 Message

CITYSCAPE

Community Transformation on the Horizon

As you continue to read, you'll find the story interrupted here and there with short Cityscapes. I want you to see places other than Atlanta where the local church has had a notable influence on the city. I hope you enjoy the view.

Life between Two Worlds

The drama of Scripture begins in a garden and ends in a city. It begins in a sylvan sanctuary where God himself walks in the cool of the day with his created image bearers. And it ends when the planet is remade and restored and includes within that world a "holy city" of unparalleled beauty.

What does that mean for us, for God's people who live between those two perfect worlds—the one created and the other re-created? As the future inhabitants of *that* city, how do we live in *this* city as it is today? And—dream with me for a moment—could it be *that* city is a reminder to us of God's plan for the daring acts of restoration and rescue he longs for his people to do in today's cities?

> Thus says the LORD of hosts, the God of Israel, to all the exiles whom I have sent into exile from Jerusalem to Babylon: Build houses and live in them; plant gardens and eat their produce. Take wives and have sons and daughters; take wives for your sons, and give your daughters in marriage, that they may bear sons and daughters; multiply there,

and do not decrease. But seek the welfare of the city where I have sent you into exile, and pray to the LORD on its behalf, for in its welfare you will find your welfare.

Jeremiah 29:4–7 ESV

Even though we live in it, we don't know how to define "the city," do we? Maybe that's because we are indeed exiles. We don't fit in. Christians in the suburbs often think of city ministry in distinctly old-school terms. We can't think "city" without attaching the prefix "inner" to it. We classify the faraway-and-separate downtown as a mission field, as exotic and unreachable as Khartoum or Nepal. *The Cross and the Switchblade*, dilapidated flop houses, bearded street preachers, and the LA soup kitchens of the movies are the gritty images that come to mind. The relationship between the church and Atlanta has been no different.

But times have changed, and we can't help but notice. Because of the gentrification of our poor out of the inner city and into the suburbs, and because of the immigration explosion in our suburbs, the challenges that were once confined to urban areas are now spreading all over the metro area. Urban sprawl is just that: a wide dispersal of "downtown" issues. Homelessness, crime, poverty, gangs, and other societal ills are now at the back door of the swim/tennis neighborhoods. Atlanta isn't unique in this way. Metropolitan areas across the country are now, in every sense except the architecture, cities.

This new, bigger city has long been overlooked as a potential repository for the grace and peace and mercy the church has to offer. It's just where we live. It is too close to our own back doors to be considered a viable mission field and too far away in its values and culture to be a "safe" investment. It is like the distant cousin who shows up at Thanksgiving and no one in the family knows what to do with him. We've not been sure how to act toward the city, what to do with it or for it. But we do know our well-being is inextricably linked with the city's.

Seek the welfare of the city where I have sent you into exile, and pray to the LORD on its behalf, for in its welfare you will find your welfare.

Jeremiah 29:7 ESV

A Tale of Three Cities

In 2004, I visited four cities: Dallas, Houston, Fresno, and Boulder. I wanted to see what community transformation looked like in other locations. I conducted phone interviews with leaders in ten other cities: San Francisco, Minneapolis/St. Paul, Cincinnati, Milwaukee, Portland, Oregon, Little Rock, St. Louis, New York, Memphis, and Corvallis, Oregon. At Perimeter Church, we were already committed to contributing to the welfare of our twelve-mile radius in the city of Atlanta. The groundwork had already been laid for Unite!, but I wanted to be better informed and more deeply inspired. I wanted a firsthand look at community transformation in other cities. I took a two-month sabbatical to do my research. It was well worth the halt in my own life and in our community transformation efforts.

I found a community within these communities. I found kindred spirits all going the same direction we were going. This view through a wider lens not only captivated me but has guided me ever since. And it has given me ongoing relationships with like-minded leaders. As I talked with these innovators, these godly lovers of their own cities, little did I know I was about to share in their adventures right here in Atlanta. The welfare of our city was going to change. And with it, inevitably, ours would too.

I'd like to draw attention to three cities in particular—Knoxville, Long Beach, and Little Rock. Like a searchlight sweeping its bright beam across the late-night sky, their skylines broadcast a message the church needs to see: *You can do this.* These cities are unique among the 150 or so cities with city-reaching ministries by evangelical groups because they boast a city-reaching movement led by *local churches.* The staffs of these churches in Knoxville, Long Beach, and Little Rock are providing leadership. They are the catalysts for community transformation. Perhaps the local church—not just its sophisticated parachurch counterpart—needs the reminder that the welfare of the city is our responsibility, our privilege. And it is our *possibility.* I've seen it in Knoxville, in Long Beach, in Little Rock. And I'm seeing it in Atlanta. The church can do this. The local church can send echoes of the future city of the King into the city of today.

Seek the welfare of the city.

Jeremiah 29:7 ESV

The axis of the earth sticks out visibly through the centre of each and every town or city.

Oliver Wendell Holmes Sr.

The Man came alive—a living soul! Then GOD planted a garden in Eden, in the east. He put the Man he had just made in it. GOD made all kinds of trees grow from the ground, trees beautiful to look at and good to eat. The Tree-of-Life was in the middle of the garden, also the Tree-of-Knowledge-of-Good-and-Evil.

Genesis 2:7–9 Message

The one who conquers, I will make him a pillar in the temple of my God. Never shall he go out of it, and I will write on him the name of my God, and the name of the city of my God, the new Jerusalem, which comes down from my God out of heaven, and my own new name.

Revelation 3:12 ESV

3

Big Questions with Big Answers

Where Are We Going?

Vacation time. It's two months away, so your family gathers in the den one night after dinner to make plans. Dad will book the flights. Mom will book the hotel. Your daughter is in charge of entertainment, and your son, the picky eater, will make the restaurant reservations. The big day arrives, and you quickly discover a problem. You hand out plane tickets to Maui. Your wife has booked hotel rooms in Vail. Your daughter shows up wearing Minnie Mouse ears and clutching all-day passes to Disney. Your son is excited about eating burgers and fries two nights in a row at the Hard Rock Café in New York. Your suitcases are filled with an ambiguous assortment of ski clothes, blue jeans, and bathing suits. Two months ago, while you were gathered together in the den, you never asked the question, Where are we going? You agreed on the idea of a vacation. You delegated responsibilities. You even put it on the calendar. But you could have precluded a trunkful of issues if you had just asked, Where are we going?

Beholding God—Our Context

The most famous road trip of all time was also one of the first collaborative missions of God's people. Moses was a leader who listened long and hard enough to hear the answer to the big question: Where are we going? In his case, Moses never had to ask; God told him outright. But it's important to note that Moses continually cultivated the kind of communication with God that made hearing him speak possible. Moses was open to what God had to say, whether he spoke out of the flames of an inconsumable bush in the desert, from the dark recesses of a tent, in the smoky crevice of a mountainside, or through the wisdom of a consultant like Aaron or his own father-in-law.

Scripture paints a brief but intriguing picture of a meeting Moses called with other leaders, Aaron, his sons, and seventy elders: "They beheld God, and ate and drank" (Exod. 24:11 ESV). Yes, this referred to physical sight, real food, and actual drink, but it is also a beautiful picture of leaders gathering to hear what God has to say to them. They partake of the Divine Nature in the context of fellowship. Movements that spring from this kind of interaction between God and his people, and his people with each other, reflect the one who speaks in unfolding glory.

Step-by-step—detours included—God's people marched toward their answer to Where are we going? Step-by-step, like the gradual opening of the compactly creased sections of a map, the journey unfolded. We see it in retrospect on the pages of Scripture, but Moses *lived* it day by day, step-by-step. Like Moses, we sometimes wonder how our own fuzzy itinerary will come into focus.

Beholding the Vision—Imagining the Future

God had called us too. Our leaders, from the top down, burned with a desire to extend the hands of Perimeter Church into the community. But how was the plan going to unfold? What in the world was it going to look like? *Where were we going?*

Our leaders didn't appoint a task force or set a plan in motion until they had some answers. They wanted to know: Where are we going? To begin answering that question, Randy and a group of key staff members met with a group of consultants who knew Perimeter Church well and understood the general direction we wanted to go. Following their direction, the staff members started with solitude. Each leader spent a season of time alone, away from their cell phones and computers and commitments, seeking God and asking him, Where are we going? What will it look like when we get there? What does it mean to transform a community? What if we turn our hearts inside out to serve the least and the lost? Each man wrote his input on 3 x 5 cards. Just to give you a taste for this stage of development, here are a few of the comments written on the cards. Note the range of topics.

About the poor areas of our city . . .

- vision for Chamblee/Doraville ethnic congregations with ethnic pastors and leaders
- four inner-city, low-income ministries started and supported and growing toward self-supporting
- fifteen to twenty families who have moved into "needy" areas for ministry
- two hundred teams of eight people who are involved in community ministry

About prayer . . .

- while we disagree in our theological discussions, we agree when we are on our knees together
- see every member praying for at least one person, ministry, situation, or problem of "the least"
- a prayer movement in subdivisions/communities/workplaces that ignores church affiliation and focuses on reaching the lost

About mercy ministry . . .

- church "enfranchises" members to serve—Perimeter is known for unleashing the enterprising nature of its members, but excellent support for fledgling ministries is chosen
- church is known for humility, innovation, and the unusual ability to tap the greatest gifts of members to serve God

- members share a crusader mentality and focus less on compliance with perceived church norms and more on finding some way to join in what God is doing

About fact-based research . . .

- determining needs in the community—initial and ongoing research
- survey—what needs do you see to which you wish this church were in ministry
- categorize identified needs
- people watching news, reading papers, and discerning needs

About attitude changes . . .

- I believed a local radio host when he said all poor people are just lazy. Then in church I heard about Emma, a black single parent who works two jobs at minimum wage. She lost one because she couldn't get to work. That was three years ago. Now I am on the MARTA (Metro Atlanta Rapid Transit Authority) board.

About events . . .

- Perimeter Church has just held its annual "city passion" weekend, with worship services focused on presenting an overall vision for the city and hundreds of members dedicating one weekend for service in one city

The mosaic of these cards (I have quoted only a few of many), gathered like bright shards of colored glass into an evolving work of art, is what eventually became Unite!

The product of this stage of the process was a document, not a spreadsheet of steps in a complicated strategy or the minutes from our last meeting. We crafted a special edition of *The Bridge*, Perimeter's monthly church newsletter.

About this same time the staff and elders of Perimeter read Robert Lewis's book *The Church of Irresistible Influence*. The bridge

Visionaries and Implementers

Visionaries speak a language of passion, of broad strokes, of wide proportions, and nearly impossible dreams. Once infected with a vision, they are ready—right now—to pursue it. They tend to ignore the potential pitfalls. They might scoff at those pitfalls if someone has the guts to suggest them. They may think pitfalls make the vision more compelling. Their juices flow when the going gets tough, or even a little crazy. And crazy is just what others call them.

Implementers pick up the vision where the visionary's impassioned speeches leave off. With the visionary's arm draped over their shoulders, the implementers stand at point A and plot the trajectory to point B. They envision not the glorious end (although they get it, they really do) but the dangers and problems along the way. They plan for them, they strategize them away, and they have the audacity to adjust the vision to doable proportions.

Visionaries speak with passion in broad strokes. They propose the What if? questions that stir our hearts. They see the glory of a rising sun on the horizon. Implementers see the horizon and immediately plot the practical ways to get there. With the blending of both languages, we can do more than just look ahead. We can surge forward.

metaphor in the book touched us in a profound way, so the cover of our newsletter featured a photograph of a towering red bridge that spanned the choppy waters of a bay and reached a stark mountainside. We wanted to build such a bridge into our community. We were committed to becoming a bridge to our city. We refused to be an island. The subtitle of the newsletter read "Transformed Lives for Transformed Communities."

We placed this edition of *The Bridge* in every seat on a Sunday morning and waited for a reaction. Here's the twist: We wrote the entire edition in the present tense but dated it five years in the future, February 2007. We wondered if anyone would notice. *The Bridge* was simply a document of our dream. It was our answer to Where are we going? as if we had already arrived. It not only answered that question but also went one step farther and asked, What if we got there? It was the edition of *The Bridge* we hoped to publish in five years. As it turns out, it was pretty close.

"Celebrating and Extending" was the headline. We hoped our people would notice the edition date in the top right corner, February 2007, and know it wasn't a typo. The "news article" proclaimed it rather dramatically:

> Involvement in mercy service has become an integral part of our discipleship curriculum. During Atlanta Passion Week members identify community needs, which are compiled, categorized, and then used to create new service opportunities. . . . Atlanta Passion Week concluded with thousands of our members joining believers from over 400 Atlanta churches for Sharefest 2007. . . . 350 refugees signed up for ESL (English as a Second Language) classes to be held in community churches. . . . Thousands of pounds of food were collected, filling the shelves of food cooperatives in the city. . . . 15 churches and 35 schools were repainted and repaired.

In 2006, one year shy of the five-year picture painted in *The Bridge*, we were amazed by the number of stories we had to tell. The unimaginable was indeed unfolding before our eyes. One part of our vision was described in the newsletter as an annual weekend of "involvement in mercy service" called Sharefest. In 2003, the first event—we decided to call it Compassion in Action Weekend—began with nine hundred volunteers from Perimeter Church and many more from other churches involved in community outreach. Four years down the road, the number of volunteers from our church alone who participated in Compassion in Action was twenty-three hundred. These volunteers were involved in 120 service projects. That translated to 500 bags of groceries, 225 pints of blood donated (each pint with the potential of saving three lives), 122 packages of diapers, and 85 filled school backpacks. Through several family ministries, we impacted approximately five thousand families in our area.

In the meantime, something else occurred that was equally unimaginable. In August of 2005, Hurricane Katrina ripped through the Gulf of Mexico and created a swath of suffering unlike any our nation had endured for a century. The homeless, the injured, the hungry, the widows, and the orphans pressed into Atlanta like a tidal wave.

Unite! was by then a functioning entity, and, through it, churches all over our area were among the first responders. When Katrina occurred, *Atlanta Journal-Constitution* reporter Bill Osinski saw what Unite! was doing, calling it a "coalition of more than 70 churches in

Gwinnett, Fulton, and Cobb counties." He recognized our ability to respond quickly and effectively to the needs. One Unite! church—Victory World Church—established a program that paired small groups with families of Katrina. Osinski wrote about the impact on one family in particular:

> Working through a church-sponsored program called Friends and Families, the residents have assisted the Lain family with things like job hunting, arranging for a donated used car and furnishing their new apartments. . . . Unite has taken the Friends and Families program, initiated at Victory World Church in Norcross, and encouraged its member churches to advocate participation.[1]

Because of Unite! partnerships, we were able to put a plan together with other churches instead of each of us doing our own thing. The result was that Unite! churches assisted over one thousand families with housing, transportation, employment, and medical needs. Most importantly, volunteers and staff from these churches made friendships with hundreds of displaced victims of Katrina. In addition, we sent work teams made up of people from various churches to the Mississippi and Louisiana coasts. The body of Christ not only worked together harmoniously but also learned a lot about working within the public, private, and social sectors for the good of the community.

We were witnessing the marriage of a monumental need and a mammoth movement of churches. By the time Katrina hit, Unite! had already created a coalition of churches and ministries that made Atlanta a haven. Sure, Christians would have responded anyway, but the groundwork of Unite! meant we could do so less haphazardly and as a unified front.

And we weren't even to 2007 yet. But it wouldn't be long.

Think about It

What is . . .

What have you or your church done to hear from God about your vision and direction? What is written down? What is the process by which you share it with your church leadership and the overall church?

What could be . . .

Write a story or an article about your church dated five years in the future. Describe in detail what it might look like if your church became a church of influence in your community.

What will be . . .

What are the strategic steps you need to take in order to:

- hear from God about his vision for your church and your city?
- document a compelling vision for where you are going?
- clearly articulate the vision to as many people in your church as possible?

What we did . . .

If you were to plot our initial steps on a linear trajectory, it might look something like this:

1. With our pastor leading the way, our hearts are stirred to become a church of influence in the community.
2. Key leaders spend time apart to pray and record their prayer-engendered ideas on 3 x 5 cards.
3. These leaders write a vision article outlining what they hope to see happen in five years and publish it in the Perimeter Church newsletter.
4. Those same key leaders gather to determine the next steps.
5. The church forms a Mercy Ministry Task Force that meets for nine months to set the details of the plan in motion.[2]

Picture This

A bridge is many things: a daring act, a visionary work of art, a way to get from here to there.

The Niagara Falls Suspension Bridge qualifies as all of the above. It is the seventh of ten bridges designed by John Roebling. The tenth and last was the Brooklyn Bridge with a span, at 1,595 feet, longer than any other bridge he designed. Roebling was not just a civil engineer; he was a risk taker. At least that's what many considered him to be: "When Roebling first proposed a suspension bridge across the great Niagara Gorge, it came as no great surprise that most people were putting their money on the gorge, not the bridge. The chasm was simply too great, too terrible."[3]

Thanks to Roebling, Niagara Falls now boasts a bridge across its treacherous waters. The risk paid off. What many considered impossible proved possible.

From the beginning, Robert Lewis and Fellowship Bible Church influenced us to build bridges. Daring bridges. Strategic bridges. If they could build a bridge to reach the least and the lost with the transforming power of the cross, so could we. If they had found a way across a chasm that "was simply too great, too terrible," then we could too.

We build too many walls and not enough bridges.

Isaac Newton

You'll be known as those who can fix anything, restore old ruins, rebuild and renovate, make the community livable again.

Isaiah 58:12 Message

45

New York City:

Lessons about Prayer from the Big Apple

A History of Prayer and Influence

If any city in the United States can track its spiritual heritage along a time line of organized, corporate prayer, New York City can. Jonathan Edwards coined the phrase "concerts of prayer" in 1747 to describe Christians coming together in visible unity and spiritual agreement. Under Edwards's leadership, congregations gathered every quarter to pray for the city and our nation. Many say the First Great Awakening began in the crucible of those local prayer meetings.

In 1857, New York businessman Jeremiah Lamphier instituted noontime prayer meetings on Fulton Street in Manhattan. Those meetings grew to include over one thousand business leaders, and again church historians believe they were instrumental in launching the Third Great Awakening, in which two million people in our nation came to faith.

But revival hasn't been the only fruit of New York's fervent prayers. Movements founded in New York like the Salvation Army and the Christian and Missionary Alliance were birthed during this period. In 1888, the presence of the Student Volunteer Movement in New York City motivated twenty-five thousand young people to enter missions in the next forty years.

Prayer. It can change hearts. And it can change history.

New York's history of prayer continued. In June 1987, Mac Pier met Ted Gandy and Aida Force from Here's Life Inner City, the urban ministry arm of Campus Crusade for Christ. The three planned their first prayer meeting in February of 1988, hoping sixteen churches and two hundred people would come. More than seventy churches attended. By September of 1989, seven regions of Greater New York were hosting their own concerts of prayer led by local pastors. These concerts of prayer evolved into annual National Day of Prayer events, held in as many as twenty-six locations at one time.

In 1990, the first official Concert of Prayer led by Concerts of Prayer International was held at the Brooklyn Tabernacle. At that gathering, four hundred pastors from a diverse mix of denominations met together to intercede for their city and the world. In 1995, area churches began to pray one day each month for the region, the nation, and the world via the Lord's Watch Prayer Vigil. Once again, personal spiritual transformation wasn't the only outcome. Between 1995 and 2000, the murder rate in New York City dropped 70 percent, making it the safest city in America of more than one million people.

If you ask the leaders of Concerts of Prayer of Greater New York (COPGNY) why they do what they do, you can hear the heartbeat of Jonathan Edwards and echoes of our country's largest city's spiritual past: "Our mission is to mobilize pastors and leaders into movements of united prayer, church growth, and global compassion. . . . Our vision is to see God heal broken cities through passionate leadership and culturally relevant churches."[4]

Teaching a City How to Pray

What strikes me about the current work of prayer in New York is not just that so many gather so often to pray but that the leaders of COPGNY are intentional about educating and enabling the body of Christ to pray. We all know how hard it is to pray, to actually do it. No one book or teaching or seminar can make it any easier. No one can alter the task so we won't ever struggle with it. But the leaders of COPGNY do all they can to make prayer doable. They don't dumb it down; if anything, they expand prayer to bigger proportions. In their monthly Lord's Watch guides, they encourage big prayers for the big needs of a big city and beyond. They highlight specific regional, national, and international prayer requests, all in the context of a huge heart for the cause of Christ. The following is the prayer guide outlined in each edition of the Lord's Watch publications:

Revival in the Church—Jesus, give us your tears for our cities.

Reconciliation—Jesus, be our peace between races and churches.

Reformation in Society—Jesus, be the protector of our cities.

Reaching Outward—Jesus, blessed is the King who comes!

Those who pray are encouraged to "REFLECT—on the Scripture verses you have read and how that has guided your prayers. REMAIN—in the presence of the Lord allowing His Spirit ample time to speak to you. RECORD—what God says to you. REPORT—testify of answered prayer."

But these intensely intimate prayer watches aren't the only way to pray corporately in New York City. Every year in June, approximately ten thousand intercessors and four hundred churches conduct a prayer walk throughout all two hundred zip codes of the city. COPGNY facilitates gatherings all over the city for the National Day of Prayer each year. They also host an annual Pastors' Prayer Summit for senior pastors, ministry teams, prayer coordinators, church planters, youth pastors, and their spouses. And they even network with believing marathoners who run the New York Marathon, inviting them to pray.

The people at COPGNY aren't content to spur churches on to prayer and leave it at that. They understand the need to act on their prayers, to do something about the issues on God's heart that fill their prayer logs. Not long ago they formed the Church Multiplication Alliance in order to accelerate the church-planting movement in metro New York by increasing the number of new churches and supporting them through prayer, training, and funding. By using the same gifts that have helped them organize and propel God's people into prayer, they now offer the following help to new church plants:

- training opportunities for potential and active church planters
- opportunities to hear from dynamic speakers and to network and pray with other church planters from around metro New York at quarterly events

- grants for qualified new churches
- regular communication and prayer support in the form of an e-newsletter
- shared information such as demographics research and best practices

COPGNY birthed the NYC Leadership Center in 2007 to lead the training and collaborative dimensions of the movement.[5] COPGNY and NYCLC share offices and support staff. They also partner with other churches, including Redeemer Presbyterian Church and its Redeemer Church Planting Center.[6] September 2009 research indicated that 39 percent of all evangelical churches in midtown Manhattan were started since 2001—the fruit of praying and collaborating with others who share the same vision.

Prayer is as natural an expression of faith as breathing is of life.

Jonathan Edwards

To pray, I think, does not mean to think about God in contrast to thinking about other things, or to spend time with God instead of spending time with other people. Rather, it means to think and live in the presence of God. All our actions must have their origin in prayer. Prayer is not an isolated activity; it takes place in the midst of all the things and affairs that keep us active. In prayer a "self-centered monologue" becomes a "God-centered dialogue."

Henri Nouwen

Call to me and I will answer you. I'll tell you marvelous and wondrous things that you could never figure out on your own.

Jeremiah 33:3 Message

Going into the Temple he began to throw out everyone who had set up shop, selling everything and anything. He said, "It's written in Scripture, My house is a house of prayer; You have turned it into a religious bazaar."

Luke 19:45–46 Message

4

Diagram of a Dream

Inventing the Wheel

It's vacation time again. This time you all agree on your destination: Disney. You and the family live in Detroit, so it's going to be one long road trip. You lost a lot of money in cancellations last year, so flying is out of the question. But you figure your family can experience more togetherness in the car. You fill the car with pillows and enough snacks to make it at least to the first pit stop, and you type Orlando into your GPS. The only problem is you can't get out of first gear.

You could turn on your flashers and drive in the slow lane the whole way, but your daughter's Minnie Mouse ears will be wilted by the time you get to Ohio. Unless you have the life span of Methuselah and the patience of Job, it's just not gonna happen.

Going the distance in the wrong gear is an unparalleled lesson in frustration . . . until you consider trying it in neutral. Now *that's* beyond frustrating; it's futile. (Hint: it's never downhill all the way.)

That's what vision is without action—you're stuck in neutral. Sure, you have the map and the munchies and the excited chatter about the trip, but you're not getting anywhere until you move. If you're ready to move, first gear is where you have to start. Then second. Then third. Try it any other way and the engine will stall. And then you're back to square one: a standstill. You long for the teeth-rattling thrill of the open road and fifth gear. You know that's how races are won. But you also know the only way to get there: from the slow promise of first.

Our church was ready to roll. We had a clear answer to the Where are we going? question. We were dreaming of the open road. We had begun asking the What if? questions: What if we refused to limit our growth as a church to the head and the heart and focused on the hand? What if we looked at our twenty-five-year track record and, instead of standing back to admire the view, looked forward to what God had in store for the future? What if we extended our hands to the community? What if we pursued justice and mercy? What if? was on our horizon in a big way.

The What if? questions stir up excitement, but that's not all. They indicate readiness. The very fact that we were asking them meant we were ready for the *next* important question: What now? What now? is where great movements really begin.

Back up and answer a few more What if? questions. What if Mother Teresa had merely observed the poor in Calcutta's slums and never asked What now? She may have spent the remaining sixty-six years of her life as a geography teacher instead of the leader of the most innovative and massive charity movement in all of India. What if John Wesley had returned from a disastrous trip to the colonies and never asked What now? Would the fiery beginnings of Methodism have happened at all? What if these great leaders had allowed the What if? question to do nothing more in their hearts than create discontentment?

The realm of What if? is thrilling. It invites dreams of expansion and adventure. What now? territory, on the other hand, can border on tedious. It is the backstory to the drama, the operations manual no one really reads, the preface most people skip over. But it is necessary. Without it, What if? dreams will never be fulfilled. As a church, we had to take some first steps to put our vision into gear. The first steps represented our unique trajectory into community ministry. Our first steps were unique to us because of where we were and where we were going. No other church will or should do it our way because no other church is exactly where we were.

Perhaps the most useful information here is not *what* we did but *that* we did it. Movements, unlike most automobiles, don't shift gears automatically.

Planning

We needed a paradigm shift—the kind of about-face that is a close cousin to repentance. We needed a change, and a fairly major one at that. Like most churches of our size, Perimeter could have a fluorescent orange "Caution: We Make Wide Turns" sign posted on the front door. Even the slightest change takes time. It's not that our people are stubborn; it's just that we are a big group and big groups move slowly. Big or small, even the most passionate visionaries must begin in first gear.

In September 2001, we formed a Mercy Ministry Task Force made up of a dozen men and women, mostly laypeople and a few staff members, all with a vested interest in the success of the new ministry. Their task: priming the pump for action. With an understanding of the delicate balance between preparation and productivity, they began praying and discussing the direction God was leading our church. From the beginning this group was supported by our pastor and top leadership. Along with our consultants, the group met monthly for nearly nine months to develop the plan. It was the ministry's gestation period. And like the nine months before a new baby arrives, it was as essential as it was tedious.

The task force acted in accordance with its name. Members translated vision into tasks, turned the dream into something doable. They wrestled with issues like infrastructure and geographic focus. In many ways, they invented the wheel so no one would have to do so down the road. They also advised us as we began to travel that road. They gave us clear directions in the following areas:

partnering
positioning
research
education
staffing

Partnering

Moses and a group of key leaders heard from God and answered the Where are we going? question for the Israelites in their trek from Egypt to the Promised Land. The answer to Where are we going? included more than a destination. It included a building plan: God gave Moses detailed instructions for the tabernacle, a moveable temple for worship. The people were given the opportunity to be involved in the building of the tabernacle by bringing raw materials for the job. They were not conscripted by Moses nor obligated in any way. Each Israelite "whose heart stirred him, and everyone whose spirit moved him" brought offerings. The project was completed by those "who were of a willing heart" (Exod. 35:21–22 ESV).

Perhaps the Israelites noticed the eerie similarity of this offering to the one they had made not too many days before. In Exodus 32, this same group of people formed an impatient mob while waiting for Moses to come down from Mount Sinai. They freely handed over their jewelry to Aaron and urged him to produce a god, any god, for them. This "offering" was not much different from the one described in Exodus 35, really, unless you consider the reason for the latter offering: a vision given by God and cast by their leader. And the result of that second offering was a work of art. Instead of Aaron's bovine sculpture haphazardly created under duress, the materials brought to Moses were crafted into a tabernacle that exactly reflected God's purposes. The first offering was a knee-jerk reaction to a perceived spiritual need. The second was an obedient response to God's call to action.

At first our desire was to "get out there" in the community. We weren't sure what that meant or what it would eventually look like, but we had willing hearts, kindled toward action by God.

We were stirred by some pretty big themes, like justice and mercy. The least and the lost can be called "the masses" for good reason—they are an overwhelmingly large group. Community transformation is a daunting task. Isolate one subgroup and look—really look—at the needs, and even the calmest strategist can lose it. Knee-jerk reactions come easily. As we began to see the face of need, the "willing heart" part wasn't difficult, but knowing when and how to act was.

It would have been easy to plow ahead with our vision without the necessary skill to do so. Sure, we could have addressed the needs ourselves, but zeal without the right tools could have caused all kinds of problems. The task force set a clear strategy in motion, and it was a sound one. Their plan enabled us to think objectively about very emotional issues.

To do big things in the world, the raw material of a willing heart is just not enough. Moses took the gold and silver and bronze given by willing participants and handed it over to skilled artisans. Only in the hands of the experts could final touches be made that would complete the work of art. These skilled workers were filled by God's Spirit with "ability and intelligence, with knowledge and all craftsmanship" (Exod. 31:3 ESV).

There were already many strong organizations in Atlanta specializing in ways we never could. They were the artisans, the specialists who knew far more than we did about their ministry specialty. One pivotal decision the task force made was to recommend *partnering* with existing ministries rather than establishing new ones. This proved to be a wise direction. It allowed our people to connect more quickly with the hurting community.

A Context for Partnership

The task force didn't recommend partnering without also recommending some basic parameters for those partnerships. As we began to build relationships with other churches and ministries, we were encouraged to overlook our differences except for the ones that really mattered. As an objective means of determining our common ground with other believers, Unite! adopted the Lausanne Covenant. From the beginning, we recognized the need to agree on the essentials of the Christian faith with those who shared the work. A statement of faith helped us to determine which beliefs were most important and nonnegotiable.

The Lausanne Covenant is a broadly evangelical document that strikes a balance between both word and deed ministry. It was written and adopted in 1974 at the International Congress on World Evangelization in Lausanne, Switzerland. It represents the synergy of 150 Christian leaders from all over the world who were committed,

As Perimeter began to form partnerships in the community, we developed a short list of criteria to help us evaluate potential relationships.

Perimeter's Criteria for Partnerships

1. We will initially focus on partnerships within the twelve-mile radius.
2. We will focus on relational partnerships. We will not give money until a lay leader and a number of our people are involved with the partner (people before money).
3. We will focus on partners who are addressing needs within our four major areas of focus.
4. We will give preference to partners who allow both word and deed ministry.
5. We will give preference to partners who focus on restoration and development of people as opposed to relief (but we will do both).
6. We will assess the return on our investment with partners—consistent with biblical parables of the soils and talents—as a way to select partners.
7. Partners must have a proven track record at the leadership level.
8. Partners must not violate biblical ethics.
9. Partners must be open to financial accountability.
10. Our preferred strategy will be to partner with an existing ministry/organization, but we may start teams that focus on needs that are not being addressed by ministries.

From the beginning, we decided we would not enter into a partnership until we had a key lay leader or leadership team that would serve as the liaison between the partner and the church. These lay leaders would act as champions for the partner to the church and would be responsible for mobilizing the church to work with the partner. The success of any partnership was usually dependent on this lay leadership.

just as we were now, to taking the transformational Good News of Christ into the world. In this covenant, we found a way to articulate not only our common beliefs but also our common purpose.[1]

Actually Doing It

Sometimes the need just about yanked our heartstrings clean off. It was hard to stay with the program when the desire to jump into a particular need was so strong.

Here's an example: children. Hungry, abused children. Fatherless children. Children sold in our own city for sex. As we began to see the needs of children, we staggered under them. The mayor of Atlanta conducted research about sex trafficking in our city. The findings were disturbing. How could we address this? How could we not? How could we find these girls, rescue them, essentially parent them, and love them?

We were a flagship church after all. Big enough to sic some of our best leaders on this issue alone and tackle it. Big enough to raise the money to fund it, to get out there and do it. And do it now.

Yet the plan was in place. As directed by the task force from the beginning, we began to search for specialists who knew more about children's issues, including sex trafficking—firsthand—than we could hope to learn. We found exactly what we were looking for in an organization called Wellspring Living.[2] We didn't need a formal introduction to Wellspring. We were already partners with them and involved in their women's program. This capable, compassionate ministry had made great strides in its mission to "change our world by changing hers." The people at Wellspring knew how to skillfully love young women in need. Like us, they were moved to respond to the issue of sex trafficking the moment they heard about it. They began to develop restoration programs and housing for child victims of prostitution and abuse. They were adept at training staff and developing material. They knew how to work with existing child service organizations to impact the lives of young girls (ages twelve to seventeen) whose lives were in ruins because of forced prostitution. They were already *doing* what was in our hearts to do. Why not join them?

Our decision to partner with those who are skilled has paid off. Our affiliation with other churches and ministries has created an apprenticeship relationship between willing workers and those groups capable of training them and putting them into ministry roles.

Eventually we were able to help other initiatives get started. Along with several other Unite! churches, we started Street GRACE (Galvanizing Resources Against Child Exploitation), a nondenominational alliance of churches dedicated to supporting and allying with individuals and organizations that are working toward eliminating the commercial sexual exploitation of children. While Wellspring's aim is to find girls who have been devastated by sex trafficking and offer hands-on healing, Street GRACE works to eliminate the problem through prevention, intervention, and restoration. Both groups share the same heart—to end the abuse of children. We wanted to mobilize the churches in our community in both ways. We wanted to support organizations that are on the front lines with the girls, and we wanted to help mobilize churches to get in the game to fight this horrible injustice in our culture. These two ministries have enabled us to do that. As we partnered with others, we learned how to get involved on every level of a need. A big impact just got bigger.

Positioning

During the 1990s, Perimeter Church pursued ministry in downtown Atlanta. Because Atlanta is a city that literally defines the term *urban sprawl*, "downtown" seemed like a separate continent to many of our people. Traffic, distance, and time are difficult hurdles to engaging the city in ministry. The inner city of Atlanta, to many who live outside it in the suburbs, is simply too far away, too removed. We wanted to reach beyond our own walls, but we didn't get far before our spotlight dimmed because the scope was so diffused and distant. That doesn't mean we won't continue to attempt great things for God inside the city, but it quickly became evident that our strategy needed a narrower focus.

The task force made the important decision to center our attention on the twelve-mile radius of the church. It is no accident that we are where we are. In fact, our location is part of our God-given stewardship. Our position on the map is a resource in itself.

Research

We asked two seminary students to research the region during the summer of 2002. They conducted demographic research as well as interviews with individuals, groups, and organizations in the community. They discovered needs and the groups that were effectively meeting those needs. Many of the issues present in our suburban pocket of Atlanta were mirror images of the city issues. The "needs of the city" were closer than we realized. The research, while disturbing, gave us confidence that we were on the right track.

Their findings not only confirmed our decision to focus on our part of suburban Atlanta but also led us to key people and organizations so that the work of building relationships in the community was begun immediately. We could proceed knowing we weren't guessing or making false assumptions about our own neighbors.

We traded a telescope for a microscope. Once we honed in on the twelve-mile radius unique to us, we began to see our community with new eyes: the public school system, the food pantries serving our area, the apartments, the youth detention centers. This strategy kept our mission from being "out there" and brought it into focus as decidedly "in here."

We have also continued a tradition of ongoing research. Our suburban context is a town called Duluth, Georgia. While the initial research was helpful at the time, it covered a broad area that included Gwinnett County and parts of Dekalb and Fulton Counties (all within the twelve-mile radius). As we began to dive into the community, we also began to see how much we still didn't know. After the Community Outreach department was established, we commissioned another research project that focused on a narrower segment of the community in which several local churches were involved. We called on a professional research consultant to help us dig deeper.

Church surveys and focus groups concentrated on our Gwinnett County town of nearly twenty-five thousand people. The research also covered various channels of cultural influence such as education, government, media, arts and entertainment, health care, the judicial arena, business, and nonprofit organizations. The next phase centered on analysis, writing, and determining collaborative opportunities for the future. As the initiator of the research, we positioned ourselves as servants to the community. By the end of our year-long Duluth Research Project, we zeroed in on several projects that the Duluth community could work on together.[3] This joint research approach can be reproduced in any city.

It is important to note here that Perimeter Church did not abandon its heart for world missions in the formation of Community Outreach and Unite! Parallel to our ministry to our local community is an equally intentional global outreach. In fact, our Global Outreach department, like Community Outreach and Unite!, places a high value on life-on-life missional discipleship. Members are also applying what Unite! has learned about city collaboration in their work with churches in strategic global cities.

Education

Like a new believer with a big, bursting heart, we needed something more than our passion if we were going to establish a viable ministry. We needed to learn, to be discipled, and to connect with someone farther down the road than we were. We needed more than inspiration; we needed education. Our efforts would be immature at best, and ineffective at worst, if we neglected to learn from others.

In 2002, twenty staff members from Perimeter attended a conference called the Irresistible Church Conference at Fellowship Bible in Little Rock, Arkansas. The purpose of this annual conference is to emphasize the message of Robert Lewis's book by the same name: to outline "what it will take to reconnect your church with the community." We knew our context was different from Fellowship Bible's and our strategy would not be the same, but we wanted to learn principles that could be used in Atlanta. It was helpful to look at a model that was already accomplishing what we hoped to accomplish. At the conference and through the book *The Church of Irresistible Influence*, we found a mentor relationship.

Without learning, fossilization is just around the corner. We continue to seek out relationships with other externally focused churches with the unabashed goal of gleaning every ounce of information and help possible from them. In the process, we've discovered a movement. We are now accountable to other people out there. Some of the key groups that have enriched us along the way are:

- Leadership Network's Externally Focused Churches Community (www.leadnet.org/LC_ExternallyFocusedChurches.asp)
- The Global Learning Community (http://globallearncomm. blogspot.com)
- The Atlanta Externally Focused Churches Leadership Community (http://atllc.blogspot.com)
- Good Cities (www.goodcities.net)
- The City Impact Roundtable (www.cityreaching.com)

Disappearing Act

Vision planners met with the task force for nine months. At the end of that time, none of the original members of the committee remained. Not one.

But it's not what you're thinking. There wasn't a mutiny, there was no mass exodus of disgruntled committee members, no walkout at the end of a theological debate, no fainthearted quitting when the going got tough. It was just life.

Life happens to big churches too. The wise leader, the visionary who wants to see the vision through, will account for attrition from the beginning. God-given visions can survive wholesale shift changes if you plan well. The task force rolled out a reproducible ministry model (emphasis on the word *model*). They invented the wheel in each major area. That way, future leaders could get on with the work without having to reinvent it at every turn.

One reason the task force was a success was that it paved the way for action steps that were in no way dependent upon its members. Without realizing how imminent it would actually be, they planned for their own disappearance.

Staffing

Before the launch of Community Outreach in 2002, Perimeter did a good job equipping our people to serve inside the four walls of the church. We also equipped our members to evangelize the people in their spheres of influence. However, we had no staff or lay leaders who were focused on mobilizing our people to go outside the walls of the church to meet the needs in the community. When needs arose inside the church, our deacons were there to serve. When needs came to us from the outside, we referred them to the local food and clothing cooperatives that we supported financially.

We realized—once we embraced adding the Hand to our mission— that we simply didn't have the manpower to do what we set out to do. Our deacons did decide to widen their service to include people in need who came to us from outside the walls of our church. Commendable and possibly even feasible, but they could not also mobilize our people out into the community. Because of the size of our church *and* the size of the impact we wanted to make in the community, the task force felt that it was important to allocate staff who could give full time and attention to the work of equipping and mobilizing our people out into the community. As I have mentioned, hiring a full-time staff isn't necessary. But, if any church is to reach outside its own walls, it *is* necessary to dedicate resources and focused attention to the task. For smaller churches this may mean a strong, lay leadership team.

Think about It

What is . . .

Has your church made any significant decisions about strategy or vision for ministry to your community?

What do you currently know about your community? Has your church conducted research, or is there research available?

What are you doing to learn from other churches in other cities?

What could be . . .

Again, picture your church five years down the road. How have you benefited from strategic decisions you made this year? What were a few of those decisions, and how did you reach them?

What will be . . .

What steps does your church need to take in order to better understand your community?

Are there some churches you can plan to approach in the next six months in order to learn from them? Name one or two.

Do you currently partner with any other churches or organizations? If so, how can you better support them? If not, what steps do you need to take to begin making those relationships? What process can you put in place to evaluate your choice of partners?

What we did . . .

We appointed a Mercy Ministry Task Force. This committee met for nine months to determine exactly how we would proceed in these areas:

- partnering
- positioning

- research
- education
- staffing

For a more complete explanation of the initial key decisions the task force made and the next steps in the process, see appendix 1.

For more information about what Perimeter is currently doing, go to www.anewkindofbig.com.

Picture This

Randice-Lisa Altschul, a successful New Jersey toy inventor, was driving down the highway and talking on her cell phone. As she drove in and out of cell coverage and lost the connection over and over, she fought the urge to throw the phone out the window. And then the thought came: Why not create a disposable phone?

It is a What if? idea others may have had before, but Altschul didn't stop there. She launched immediately into What now? Although she had no experience in the field of electronics, Randice-Lisa did know about innovation. She partnered with an engineer to create the ultrathin circuitry to go in her phone. In 1999, she was issued a series of patents for the circuitry and the wireless prepaid cell phone. She called this phone "an enhanced calling card." The next step was another partnership with a local company to develop a marketing strategy.

Eventually other companies latched on to the idea and began distributing disposable phones. But Altschul is recognized as the inventor of the idea. In 2002, the phone-card-phone was named product of the year by Frost and Sullivan.[4]

An entire community has benefited from the disposable phone idea: mothers and children who need to stay in touch, the elderly who don't want to invest in monthly plans, and travelers. A What if? moment led to What now? And answering What now? led to a process. Good ideas begin that way. As they develop they expand. As others enter into the process, an idea is crafted into something important, something that works. For a mere idea to become an actual product, it cannot remain a What if? dream. Granted, it is a lot easier to complain and consider throwing your cell phone out your car window, but to solve a problem, to meet a need, *someone* must ask What now? and begin the slow process of turning a dream into a reality.

The needs in our community were huge, so huge that it would have been easy to talk about them without ever taking any of the seemingly small baby steps it took to begin meeting them. But we weren't content to stay at What if? Nothing would change if we stopped there.

> Nothing is particularly hard if you divide it into small jobs.
>
> Henry Ford

> Before anything else, preparation is the key to success.
>
> Alexander Graham Bell

> Refuse good advice and watch your plans fail; take good counsel and watch them succeed.
>
> Proverbs 15:22 Message

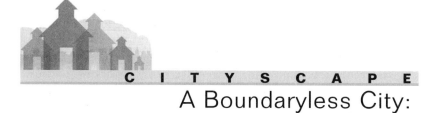

A Boundaryless City:
The Friendship Factor

We Get By with a Little Help from Our Friends

Atlanta has 285. Little Rock, 430 and 440. New York, 287. Knoxville, 475. It could be said that these circular interstate highways define the cities they encompass. Like ancient cities that relied on walls to delineate their borders, we usually think of cities in terms of their boundaries. They are geographical places. But let's use a transcendent definition here: a city is a collective body of people. A community.

If Unite! is anything, it is a community. And perhaps the most rudimentary definition of a community is that it is a gathering of friends.

When the vision of Unite! first gripped me, I began to gather friends who shared that vision. Many were in Atlanta, some were not. We each understood the need to impact our cities, and we were committed to that. What drew us together, like metal filings to a central magnet, was our common purpose, not a common place. What held us together was something far more binding than a "beltway" or a "perimeter"; it was friendship. Those who were part of the literal twelve-mile radius around Perimeter Church joined in the task right here. Others influenced and encouraged from their own place of ministry.

Friendship. We all desperately need it. Sniff around any organization, any industry, any workplace and you'll discover a factor that can spell either the success or the disaster of that entity: friendship.

65

We need friends where we live. A 2007 J. D. Power study investigated the needs of apartment residents in four major cities. Their purpose: to determine what makes apartment dwellers stay put. In this highly competitive industry, resident retention is everything. Knowing the pulse of your market is vital. So what do you think lures renters to a particular apartment complex? And, more importantly, what keeps them there once they move in?

Apartment dwellers who participated in the survey cited air-conditioning and plumbing problems, pest control issues, and waste pickup troubles as major headaches. Crime in the area or poor management scored high on their "get out of this lease as soon as I can" scale. They said they chose their current apartments based on amenities like the swimming pool, laundry facilities, and fitness center. But what was the number-one factor in a resident's decision to stay? Community.[5] That's right. "If you build it, they will come" is a fantasy. "If they have friends here, they will stay" is a documented fact.

We need friends where we work too. Tom Rath, head of Gallup's Workplace and Leadership Consulting, published the results of years of research in *Vital Friends: The People You Can't Afford to Live Without*. Bottom line: Friendships help you love your job. And when you love your job, you perform better. Among other findings, Rath's research uncovered this data about friendships at work:

- Without a best friend at work, the chances of being engaged in your job are 1 in 12.
- People with at least three close friends at work are 96 percent more likely to be extremely satisfied with their life.
- Employees who have a close friendship with their manager are more than 2.5 times as likely to be satisfied with their job.[6]

What about church? Is a decision to visit a church merely a "spiritual" one for most people? Probably not. Southern Baptist head of missions Ed Stetzer was interviewed by Cathy Lynn Grossman for *USA Today* about Americans' receptivity to evangelistic contacts and outreach from a church. He cited the findings of Lifeway Research and the North American Mission Board. In a study of over fifteen thousand people, 56 percent of those surveyed said they would be willing to have a personal conversation *with a friend* about a local church.[7] Billboards, radio ads, and other means of connecting were far less appealing ways of getting their attention than a chat with a friend.

A Cause Built on Friendships

In every arena of life, the need for friendships is clear. But sometimes those of us who are leaders, who are passionately on a mission, don't get this right. Maybe that's because our cause eclipses our common sense in this area. Our cause is the magnet, the reason for gathering in the first place, our "true north." And our cause is big. It's bigger than any of us. You'd think the cause alone would be big enough, compelling enough, to keep our motors running. Not so.

A cause cannot sustain us when no relationships form around it. A cause can all too easily shrivel to nothing more than an idea, something so noble that we border on being so heavenly minded that we're of no earthly good. Build your work around a cause alone, and you may end up with nothing more than a well-oiled ministry machine. Without relationships we're acting in a vacuum.

Mac Pier, head of Concerts of Prayer in New York City, stresses that the causes that last are those built on relationships. I concur. The cause—community transformation—of Unite! gave me the gift of friendship when it was nothing more than a dream. Bryan White, a big guy, a former Buffalo Bill, and one of the pastors at Hopewell Missionary Baptist Church who dreamed with me from the beginning, has become my best friend. That connection—around our common passion for the cause of community transformation—was the pilot light that ignited our friendship. After our first Compassion in Action Weekend, when our two churches worked and worshiped together, Bryan said, "For us it's about church transformation more than community transformation. As an African-American church, we have always run to the church as our refuge. But we've got to go outside our walls and get involved where the pain of the city is. What the churches are doing through Unite! is so much on the heart of God. It's something we are privileged to be in on."

But Bryan and I share much more than a cause. We're friends. In many ways, our friendship transcends the cause. Unite! brought us together around a noble theme, but I am honored to call this noble

67

man of God my brother. That means more. We know and love each other's family. We love to hang out together. We share with each other our dreams and passions and our fears and failures. We come from different cultures, but we both have red blood in our veins. We joke with others that we are twins separated at birth. It is relationships like these that drive a movement.

Other friends have bolstered, mentored, and encouraged me along the way. When I first got into ministry as a student ministry intern, Matt Brinkley (student ministry pastor at Perimeter at the time) mentored me and taught me the value of life-on-life missional discipleship as he invested in me personally. I learned how to pastor by simply observing his life up close. He loved me and encouraged me, and I learned that real ministry is done through relationships. Matt is still one of my best friends. Drue Warner has been a friend and colaborer from the beginning. He is a primary contributor to the Community Outreach and Unite! story. Our gifts complement each other so well. Eric Swanson, author of *The Externally Focused Church*, has been a coach and mentor to me in externally focused ministry and city transformation. Eric's influence has been a common thread every step of the way. As the director of Leadership Network's Externally Focused Churches, he invited me and Perimeter to be part of the first Externally Focused Churches Leadership Community in 2004–2005. He and Sam Williams also invited me to be part of the Global Learning Community, which consists of city catalysts from all over the world. More than anything Eric has become a great friend, and I know he is there for me. Ray Williams in Little Rock, Andy Rittenhouse in Knoxville, and Eric Marsh in Long Beach are catalysts in their cities, and I have learned much from them as we have become great friends. All of these men taught me how to combine good works and Good News as the two powerful messages for community transformation.

The same kind of network of friends has developed here in Atlanta as well. In 2007, we established the Atlanta Externally Focused Churches Leadership Community (http://atllc.blogspot.com) patterned after Leadership Network's Externally Focused Church Leadership Communities. Two to four leaders from twelve Unite! churches met four times for two days each over a two-year period. We learned from each other and brought in experts on topics such as volunteer mobilization, innovation, and racial reconciliation. This was a real boost to Unite! and helped us expand to other regions. And we became friends on a deeper level.

Building Bridges

Friendships are avenues of healing as well. Bryan and I sense that our relationship has started something bigger than the two of us. As a black man and a white man doing ministry in the South, we easily could have missed each other. That's an embarrassing fact, since our churches are only a few miles apart. As Bryan says, "I wasn't looking for a white friend." But Jesus, who leads the way in friend making, knew we needed each other. And he knew the kingdom cause we both embrace would be richer, more meaningful, in the context of our friendship.

We like to think we aren't the only ones who have been enriched by our relationship. What God has done in us, he has done in his church. After our second Compassion in Action Weekend, Bryan and I both reveled in the beauty of the worship service. We knew it represented a measure of healing for our churches. I think Bryan got it right: "I sense that this wasn't a stretch for our churches to worship and serve together but more of a release into what God's people have longed to do."

> Greater love has no one than this, that one lay down his life for his friends.
>
> John 15:13 NIV

> In everyone's life, at some time, our inner fire goes out. It is then burst into flame by an encounter with another human being. We should all be thankful for those people who rekindle the inner spirit.
>
> Albert Schweitzer

> A friend knows the song in my heart and sings it to me when my memory fails.
>
> Donna Roberts, senior economist at the Economic Research Service

5

The Epic Becomes Us

Education, Poverty, Family, Justice

It begins as a tale worthy of a *Law & Order* episode: Politically powerful man discovers his wife's infidelity. Murders her. Remarries. Murders that wife too. Get inside this guy's head and you'll discover some pretty messed-up ideas. He has developed a homicidal agenda based on a strange obsession. According to our serial killer, all women are unfaithful. His solution: marry them one by one and kill them one by one. Commit the deed before sunrise the next day, before the honeymoon can even begin. He's influential, remember? So he gets away with it. Over and over.

Until he marries a woman smarter than he is. Smart *and* brave. She volunteers for the job with the expressed purpose of ending—with her wits—the wholesale slaughter of young brides. Every night for 1,001 nights, she tells her new husband a story. Every night she doesn't end the tale but stops just before the dramatic conclusion. And every night she buys herself another day of life. Tragedies, love stories, and historical drama are mixed in with poetry, philosophy, and complex descriptions of human anatomy. The commonality in each tale: suspense. Her core motif is the cliffhanger. "But wait, there's more" like you've never heard it before. I'm speaking, of course, of *The Arabian Nights* (or *One Thousand and One Nights* as it is known in Arabic).

Interestingly, the young bride's stories are told as a collection of folktales within a "frame story." The larger legend of the Persian king Shahryar and his never-ending wedding night with the bride Scheherazade provides a structure for the assortment of smaller narratives, each capable of standing alone. But they don't. They connect because—together—they communicate broader, deeper themes.

One such theme is what Persian readers would have called fate. In each story are coincidences, fulfilled destinies, often comedic encounters that remind the reader of one's dependence upon fate. As Christians, with a biblical, God-centered understanding of life, we would recognize in these tales of fate the truth of God's sovereignty contrasted with our lack of control. That's the beauty of mythic themes in art and literature: They can't help but point to God's truth.

Our Story Deepens

Our goal was community transformation. God had called Perimeter Church to impact our world by turning our hearts inside out for the least and the lost. That was our metanarrative, our overarching structure, our big picture. But what themes could be woven into the narrative? What deep thematic elements and what daring plot twists could we pursue? We knew we were in the beginning stages of a drama, and we didn't want to leave out the important chapters.

We wondered, If someone were to read our story in five years, what themes would emerge? No story can tell it all, so we began to narrow our focus. The task force made the difficult decision to stick with only four major areas of ministry, four noble causes.

We didn't shake a magic eight ball; we relied on the research we had already done to guide us. The data highlighted four people groups, or areas of need. We have made some slight adjustments over the years, but just as theme determines plot, the overall direction of our story has remained fairly intact. The current four impact areas are education, poverty, family, and justice.

Committing to education was a first step, but it was still too general. We wanted to reach kids and families, so we went to the places we knew we would find them en masse. We determined to become servants to the local public schools.

It is easy to miss the poor. We don't work where they work, live where they live, or shop where they shop. Instead of setting up false ways of relating with little expertise, we opted to come alongside organizations that knew the needs more intimately and had already strategized effective ways to help. In this way, we began intentionally, and the learning curve wasn't impossibly steep.

We discovered early on in our research that women and children in our area were a group often in crisis. We also learned there were some excellent ministries that knew how to operate in this delicate area. Over the years we have developed some partners within Perimeter Church, but we began by affiliating with others outside our church.

The research on justice issues was perhaps the most overwhelming. We learned that our city is one of the top cities in the country for sex trafficking of children. As we began to be educated about these disturbing facts, we knew we had to weave this theme into our story—not just the facts but a response to them.

These four areas overlap in many ways and are not always neatly defined categories. But focusing on these four areas has proven to be a good way to structure our partnerships and our lay leadership. We also have target outcomes in the community that are measureable in each of these four areas. We'll talk more about these in chapter 11. These outcomes spring from goals developed by Unite! churches. These targets enable us to see what actually happens in the community. They become rallying points that help people see where we are going and measure how far we have to get there.

As you can imagine, the more we studied these themes and the more they became real people, real issues, and real needs, the more we were daunted by the task before us. We were never going to be big enough. How could we craft a story big enough to contain everything that needed to happen? The more we looked outside our doors, the larger the landscape loomed. We were overwhelmed and intimidated. We were a tiny David church in a huge Goliath world.

But sometimes intimidation can be a good thing. Our pursuit of big themes enriched and enlightened us in several ways. First, we were even more convinced we needed a new kind of big. That's because, though our church was and is a megachurch, it was not big enough; though, by most standards, we had a big budget, it was not big enough either; though we had planted an impressive network of churches in the city, it was still not big enough.

We asked ourselves, What if we threw out all our provincial, proprietary thinking about church and made this about the kingdom instead? What if we joined hands with other churches and ministries? We were committed to that ideal, but the size of the task convinced us that it was the only way to get it done. If we were to make an impact, we couldn't do it alone. To tell a story like this, with big themes and a big plot, we needed a rich cast of characters.

Second, we watched the big stuff edge out the small. Churches can easily become embroiled in petty issues: carpet color, bulletin paper, committee chair appointments, etc. Compared to justice for the oppressed or food for the hungry, who had time for all that? Our chosen themes gave us perspective.

Third, we were even more persuaded that this was God's thing, not ours. Our pastor had often challenged our leadership to pursue dreams that were so big they were doomed to failure unless God was in them. We were pretty sure this was the kind of dream he meant.

You may be thinking, This is great, but when did they stop *thinking* and start *doing* something? I have to admit, there were times when I was impatient too. But I cannot emphasize enough that we were deliberately slow in our process. Remember that early question, Where are we going? We took our time finding answers to that question so that when we finally took the first steps, they were sure. Embedded in any answers to Where are we going? were the answers to Why are we going and how will we get there? We took our time answering those too. We started with themes and strategies. Then we began making overtures to churches and organizations. Thorough research takes time. Real relationships (that's what we wanted our partnerships to be) take time.

Knights in Shining Armor?

Another major theme embedded in those early decisions emerged over time. We began with a broad target group, "the least and the lost" in our community. Just who are the least and the lost in God's opinion?

Some of our people took umbrage not with the target group but with the terminology we used to describe them. As we moved toward the actual people we defined as "least" and sought out those who were "lost," we realized that they were much more than a category and we'd better learn to see them as more than a project or a program. *Least* and *lost* are biblical words. Shouldn't we discover their biblical meaning? Shouldn't we turn their meaning upside down? Why? Because that's how Jesus saw them. *Least* and *lost* were words he defined in ways the rest of the world did not.

The least are devalued by our culture: the poor, the young, the widows, the orphans, the dirty, the uneducated, the sullen and sad, the down-and-out. Jesus didn't just model a new way of thinking about the least; he taught it, he emphasized it, and he used visual aids to make sure his disciples got it:

> Jesus, knowing their thoughts [i.e., knowing our tendency to look down on the least], took a little child and had him stand beside him. Then he said to them, "Whoever welcomes this little child in my name welcomes me; and whoever welcomes me welcomes the one who sent me. For he who is least among you all—he is the greatest."
>
> Luke 9:47–48 NIV

But Jesus went farther than this illustration in defining the least. He personally identified himself as one of the least. In fact, he clearly stated that loving the least meant the same thing as loving him: "I tell you the truth, whatever you did for one of the least of these brothers of mine, you did for me" (Matt. 25:40 NIV).

It's startling but true. When we feed a hungry person (or stock the shelves of a food pantry that feeds hungry people) or clothe a homeless man (or give to a clothes closet that distributes clothing) or provide a home for a single mother and her children (or help out at a day care in a women's shelter), we are not just loving Atlanta's least, we are loving Jesus. When we understand this, it's hard not to grant dignity to those we serve. We are serving the Lord himself.

The meaning of *lost* is a little more straightforward. No one wants to be lost. Not found. Missing. Absent. AWOL. Like *least*, *lost* isn't a pretty word. Simply put, someone who doesn't know Jesus is lost. Again, it's a biblical term. But Jesus always pointed to the diamond gleaming inside the dark coal of lostness. To Jesus, lostness carried within it the promise of the exquisite joy of foundness. Finding the lost: Jesus reveled in it. He described it in ways every person with a beating heart could understand. Read his stories about finding the lost, and you can't help but conclude that lost things have immeasurable value. That's why we search for them. That's why we throw parties when they are found. The implication is clear: If you are lost and your Owner is desperate to locate you—so much so that time stands still in his heart until he finds you—then you are not only lost but also loved. We are worth more than money can buy (if that's all we were worth, our Owner would simply replace us when we wander away). You know the stories:

> Rejoice with me; I have found my lost sheep. . . .

> Rejoice with me; I have found my lost coin. . . .

> But we had to celebrate and be glad, because this brother of yours was dead and is alive again; he was lost and is found.

> Luke 15:6, 9, 32 NIV

As we redefined these terms, our hearts were turned upside down as well. We began to make sure we were, in every way, treating the least and the lost with all the dignity and respect and real love we could muster. We had to wonder if we weren't a bit too self-important. We had to work on that. And we had to ask, Is the "knight in shining armor" a biblical missions model? What were we communicating to the community if we swooped in on the imposing steed of our money and influence and expertise to "rescue" those who couldn't rescue themselves? The truth is, Jesus didn't operate that way. He was the suffering Servant. And so the question became, What does servanthood look like?

For us, it looks like anonymity. It looks like a gift with no strings attached. It looks like coming beside rather than before or behind. And it looks like partnership. Partnering with other churches and ministries has kept us from delivering a "get out of the way, we are the experts" message. It is safe to say most people we have been able to help have no idea Perimeter Church is a key leader of Compassion in Action or Unite! Joining with others has kept us from overwhelming "little people" with a "big church" offensive. Because of our partnerships, we have been able to keep service front and center—service that spotlights Jesus instead of his servants.

Perhaps the most effective way we learned these lessons was through the volunteers on the ground. The people who made sacrificial decisions that placed them right in the middle of injustice and poverty, by their example, taught us to dignify the least and to value the lost. We simply provided the backdrop; they lived the drama. Theirs are the real stories.

Ben and Julie Sawyer

When Ben and Julie Sawyer and their three children moved into Huntington Ridge Apartments in June of 2005, they weren't writing a story; they were just doing the next thing God called them to do. As Perimeter Church members, they got involved with Community Outreach and soon discovered a vast need in the apartment communities not far from the church. Perimeter hosted events and tutoring programs at Huntington Ridge, but the need required more than weekly visits. What was really called for was incarnational ministry. Like Jesus—who "became flesh and blood, and moved into the neighborhood" (John 1:14 Message)—the Sawyers realized that this community needed to experience the love of the Savior *in their midst*. And so they moved into the neighborhood, and God began to write the story.

Like all good stories, this one isn't black-and-white. It is full of irony. When Ben and Julie first moved to Atlanta, they spent one harrowing month in an extended-stay hotel. Weekly drug busts and the wail of sirens most nights convinced them this was *not* their mission field. In fact, they planned to get as far away from it as they could, as soon as they could.

Fast-forward a few years to Ben and Julie's new home at Huntington Ridge . . . across the street from that same hotel. Julie now laughs when she explains the change in her heart that compelled her to go back to a place she had vowed to avoid at all costs. What caused that change? Maybe it began as a challenge or a calling, but the force that sustained the Sawyers during their two years at Huntington Ridge was love—the love of God for them and their neighbors, and their love for the people among whom they settled.

Without that love the need would have been too staggering, too depressing. The apartment community was a village of refugees. Most were from the Oaxaca region of Mexico, and most were here illegally. Ben and Julie saw firsthand the fallout of a community in crisis. They quickly learned that their ideas about what would be helpful were misinformed and ineffective. They fully embraced the mission of community transformation, but they found it looked different from the ground.

The churches of Unite! partnered with the Sawyers by giving them resources to do that work on the ground. There was no place for children to play at Huntington Ridge. Garbage was everywhere, and the property wasn't safe. During the Compassion in Action Weekend of 2006, a team of over one hundred people donated time and money to build a new playground and rehabilitate the activity center. Their efforts went a long way toward solving problems in one community.

Talk with Ben or Julie and you'll get an education about social problems. They understand them in a unique way. Ultimately, when you live smack-dab in the middle of the people you serve, social problems begin to come into focus, and they look different. They look like people, people like Maria.

Maria was a leader among her peers at Huntington Ridge. Practically a single mom (her husband was an abusive alcoholic who lived in Mexico), self-sufficient and proud, Maria would never have asked for a handout. Two of her children attended tutoring sessions led first by Community Outreach volunteers and later by the Sawyers. One afternoon Maria's son mentioned that his mother was stressed because she couldn't pay her water bill. Julie went to see her and arranged, through several partner ministries in Community Outreach, to help with her bill.

Julie and Maria's friendship grew slowly. Eventually Maria allowed Julie to pray with her. Julie invited her to church, and she went. Maria moved out of Huntington Ridge, but the two women stayed in touch. When a Guatemalan medical missionary came to Perimeter Church and shared the gospel in what Maria called her heart language (Spanish), she responded immediately. Her son and the Sawyers' son went on a sixth-grade retreat together, where the son followed his mother's lead and accepted Christ. Julie's friend began to grow in her faith, and as she did she found a new self-assurance that permeated her life and a new purpose that kept her going. It wasn't long before Maria's new faith was put to the test.

Everyone at Huntington Ridge knew Maria's husband. He was a real charmer who had cheated death so many times it was said he had nine lives. Yet most people didn't know about his heavy drinking and the vicious way he abused Maria and the children. When he somehow made it back over the border and showed up in Atlanta, no one was surprised, and most were elated, except for Maria. Her husband's arrival created a conflict she'd not experienced before she met Christ. She now had a deeper, more protective love for her children and a more profound understanding of her own worth. She simply could not return to the life she'd had before. For four months, with the support of her new faith community, Maria lived out the grace she now knew and enforced the boundaries she had to create for her family. Her husband respected her wishes and went to live with relatives. That's where he was when he died of alcohol poisoning.

Maria struggled to live out her faith in her community during the days following her husband's death. The superstitions and traditions of her heritage didn't always fit in her newfound walk of faith. As she worked to walk in truth yet find commonality with her family in order to love them, she grew. Today Maria is a vital member of a Hispanic church that grew out of Perimeter's outreach to Huntington Ridge and other apartment communities like it. In Maria's life, the story of community transformation is complete.

What is a tale without characters? The stories in *Arabian Nights* endure because of the people, the ones who make the drama *happen*. Do we remember Shakespeare's plays because of their themes or because we can't forget Romeo or Lady Macbeth? Themes that never put on living flesh are didactic and dead. But combine a worthy theme with living, breathing characters like Maria and the Sawyers, and you have a great work, an opus, a masterpiece.

Think about It

What is . . .

What are the overarching themes that you and your church are trying to address in your community?

Do you have any dreams that are bigger than life? Is there anything you and your church long to accomplish that simply cannot be done unless God does it?

What are you and your church doing in the community to prevent the "knight in shining armor" mentality?

What could be . . .

List three potential themes you and your church could begin addressing in the community in the next six months.

- What critical factors would enable you to succeed?
- What obstacles might you face?
- What early indicators of success would encourage you to keep going?
- Five years down the road, what does success look like?

What will be . . .

What are the strategic steps you need to take to define your target themes?

What can you do to equip your people to build kingdom relationships with those in the community?

What are several action steps to take in these areas over the next six months?

What we did . . .

In the summer of 2002, Perimeter Church hired three full-time Community Outreach staff persons: a director, an associate, and an administrative assistant.

As the director of Community Outreach, I set up meetings with key leaders in other churches and ministries. I also met monthly with local missions pastors as a group.

We identified the partners in the community that best fit our criteria and were a good match for the themes we chose. The data from

The Great Commission
or the Great Conquest?

The feature film *The End of the Spear* gave moviegoers a vivid picture of Jesus-like missions. Five young missionaries, including Steve Saint's father, Nate, literally gave their lives for the men who speared them to death on the banks of the Ehuenguno River in Ecuador. Not long after the martyrdom, Steve's aunt Rachel and one of the widows, Elisabeth Elliot, chose to take the gospel deeper into the jungle to the Waodani tribe, the very people responsible for the murder of their loved ones.

Steve grew up among the Waodani and, as a child, witnessed the baptism of the men who killed his father. Two of those men baptized Steve and his sister. He was there when the seeds of a brand-new church took root.

After many years in the States, Steve returned to Ecuador. What he discovered carries a sobering message for any church hoping to make a difference in the lives of the least and the lost.

"I returned to those jungles hoping to find a flourishing and thriving church. . . . With twentieth-century resources, equipment, and training behind them, I couldn't wait to see how far they had come.

"But what I saw instead was a church that was far less functional than it had been in my mid-teens. Instead of a self-propagating, self-governing, and self-supporting church among the Waodani, there was just a collection of individual believers. I was both saddened and perplexed. What had happened?

"One snapshot explains it all. I noticed that the Waodani elders weren't baptizing new converts. My sister Kathy and I had been baptized by two men named Kimo and Dyuwi. I asked them, 'You were elders when you took Tamaya (Kathy's name in the Waodani language) and me into the water; are you still taking new God followers into the water?'

"They answered, 'The Cowodi (foreigners) take the people into the water.'"[1]

Steve Saint's contention was that the smaller, needier, "least" church is often marginalized by missionaries whose expertise, though wielded with noble intentions, communicates this message: You are not capable to lead. We can do it better. This message disregards the truth that the least are, in God's economy, the greatest.

our initial research and our chosen people groups of internationals, women and family, youth at risk, and dependents helped us determine what ministries to connect with first. In order to coordinate with Unite!'s four impact areas, we later changed our four areas of emphasis to poverty, education, family, and justice. For the most part, our partners stayed the same.

To get more information about what Perimeter is currently doing, go to www.anewkindofbig.com.

Picture This

Leitwortstil (German for "leading word style") is the "purposeful repetition of words" in a given literary piece that "usually expresses a motif or theme important to the given story." The device is used in several of Scheherazade's stories in *Arabian Nights*. It is used "to shape the constituent members of the story cycles into a coherent whole."[2]

Sometimes God speaks to us repeatedly—with a *leitwortstil*—to make his point clear. Almost like an echo across a canyon, his leading rebounds from one voice to another, but instead of dying out like a shout in empty space, it strengthens with each recurrence. That is the beauty of the body of Christ: the diverse synergy of its people. Over time the wisdom of our leaders, the advice of the task force, the findings of the researchers, and even the presenting needs of our community and the specific proficiencies of our church all came together to mark the way for us.

Community transformation. That echo still resounds. It is our clearest *leitwortstil*. It is a phrase repeated to us that we repeated to the congregation that they repeat to each other. Our means of transforming community is a secondary, recurring theme: turning our hearts inside out for the least and the lost. These are the phrases God has used, and we have echoed, "to shape the constituent members of the story cycles into a coherent whole." And what a story it has become.

Who will change old lamps for new? . . . new lamps for old?

The Arabian Nights

For the Son of Man came to find and restore the lost.

Luke 19:10 Message

6

The Human Chain

Developing Community Partnerships

If drowning is your worst nightmare, imagine the horror of drowning in subzero water beneath a layer of ice. It's a nightmare that almost came true for Frank Crawford one chilly Christmas afternoon in 1906. Despite repeated warnings from his friends, Frank skated to an area known to be treacherous in the Morris Canal between Jersey City and Easton, Pennsylvania. In true adolescent form, the seventeen-year-old showed off his skating skill, gallantly ignoring the danger. An air pocket at the deepest part of the canal was his undoing. A loud crack, a splash, and Frank was in deep trouble.

As he began to sink, Frank's buddies heard his screams for help and skated . . . to a safe distance away. Henry DaVita quickly improvised. First he sidled up to the break in the ice where his friend was struggling to stay afloat. Then he and five or six other teenagers lay on the ice, forming a human chain linked hand to ankle. Henry's first attempt to grasp Frank failed, but on the second try he was able to pull him out of the water by the shoulders. Once he was safe, the chain slowly and deliberately backed away from what could have easily been Frank Crawford's frozen grave.[1]

Rescues are hardly ever solo affairs. Policemen have partners. When two aren't enough, they call for backup. The Coast Guard doesn't send a lone diver to battle the waves and scout for survivors of a tragedy at sea. Soldiers never advance alone. Describing the scene at a fire, firefighters refer to the job "we" did. That's how it's done: as a team. The more daring the rescue, the more desperate the need, the hotter the fire, the higher the waves, the more menacing the enemy, the more teamwork is absolutely vital.

Calling for Backup

We were convinced we could not do the big job we set out to do alone. And if we were going to form a "human chain" strong enough for the daring deeds we hoped to perform, we had to call for backup. Yes, Perimeter was a megachurch with megaresources, but the needs were more mega than we were. We simply *had* to partner with groups more equipped than we could ever be if we were going to get the job done.

We became links in the chains that extend out into the community, and we're continually forging new relationships. As the old Shaker song says, we "make new friends while keeping the old," discovering both to be silver and gold. Here are just a few of the precious metal links in the ever-lengthening chain of the work of both Community Outreach and Unite! We have come to consider them our dear friends.

Hi-Hope Service Center

Mentally impaired people require specialized care. Unless you have firsthand experience with disabled adults, you may not know how to bridge the gap. It's all too easy to think of them as untouchables, an isolated subgroup in our culture that we cannot reach. Hi-Hope Service Center, located in Gwinnett County, is an organization that specializes in meeting the needs of adults with developmental disabilities. Our partnership with Hi-Hope and their group homes has given us the means to touch the untouchable. The marriage of willing volunteers and experts at Hi-Hope caused the *Gwinnett Daily Post* to take notice:

> Five years ago a yard clean-up and beautification project at our Willis House group home began. Members of the ballroom dance club

at Perimeter Church and Claire Dees, a volunteer coordinator for disability outreach at Perimeter, started this one-time project, which quickly became a biannual project.

Currently, some 30-plus volunteers show up at the home biannually to pull weeds, spread mulch, plant trees, flowers and shrubs, visit with the residents and have lunch together. Many of the residents also work alongside the volunteers while creating lasting friendships.

However, this spring Mark Dees had the wonderful idea of planting a garden. No one could have predicted the response from the volunteers. Nor could anyone have imagined the impact on the volunteers. Everyone always thinks that it is our residents that are being helped. This project is evidence that helping is a two way street.[2]

In many ways, Hi-Hope's mission statement mirrors our own: "The Hi-Hope family is energetically committed to participating in the community by building relationships, working, volunteering, collaborating with other agencies, and developing new programs to meet the changing needs of the community."[3] Just as a friendship is instantly formed when two people meet over coffee and are delighted to discover a like-mindedness, our partner relationships are shaped by a connection in our visions.

Victoria's Friends

Planting a garden at a home for the mentally impaired turned out to be a brilliant plan to build friendships with the residents there, a simple act of kindness that oiled the hinges and opened the door. But what about the fortress of the adult entertainment industry? What about the women—usually controlled by violent men—who work in that industry because it is their only option for survival?

Once again we partnered with organizations that were neither intimidated nor baffled by the seeming impossibility of rescue, and, once again, we took part in an uncomplicated plan to penetrate a complex, broken world.

One of our partners is Victoria's Friends, a local nonprofit organization specializing in ministering to women in crisis. Baskets of Love is one of their more daring ventures. Each month volunteers from Victoria's Friends take baskets to the dressing rooms of local strip clubs. On Valentine's Day children from Perimeter Church made colorful valentines to go in these baskets—each unique and beautiful, just like the women who would receive them. That month, armed with simple gifts, women boldly approached some of the most guarded establishments in Atlanta. One volunteer described the scene:

> When we arrived at the first club, I asked the bouncers for the owner. Without even looking at me, they informed me she wasn't there. They weren't going to let us in! Suddenly, a man in a three-piece suit appeared and demanded they allow us through. I felt like we had arrived at a family reunion—hugs and kisses all around! We stepped out in boldness and asked if the girls wanted prayer. They did, and they were not ashamed to ask! We even got to pray with the house mom for healing. We met a pastor's kid who had rebelled. She had read *Redeeming Love*, the book we had distributed to all the girls for Christmas, and now she is ready to return home!

Norcross Cooperative Ministry

The Norcross Cooperative Ministry (NCM) is a partner ministry devoted to meeting the emergency needs of residents in a large segment of our community. At any given moment, NCM is poised to provide food, clothing, or household items for families in need. Like most ministries of this kind, readiness for service is a continual challenge. That means they need partnering churches. It also means we get to be in on miracles of provision.

On the Wednesday before the Coop's annual Book Bag Bonanza—an event in which filled book bags are distributed to needy schoolchildren in our community—there were supplies for just three hundred bags. Not enough for the need. By Saturday, thanks to the relationship between Perimeter Church and the Coop, 733 fully loaded book bags were handed out to smiling children.

World Relief

At any given time, Atlanta is home to thousands of refugees from all over the world. An organization known as World Relief is a partner in this area of astounding, continual need. Securing jobs for refugees is just one issue in a long list. Finding a job creates a new set of needs: clothing, language, child care, and transportation. When we discovered that many refugees had found work at a chicken plant in Perry, Georgia, an almost two-hour drive from Atlanta, volunteers from Perimeter Church worked with World Relief to provide funds for a van for these newly employed refugees.

Movers and Shakers

One of our members noticed a unique need he thought he could rally others to meet. Using his personal business acumen and his connection to Perimeter Church and Unite!, he began a ministry called Movers and Shakers, which specializes in picking up and delivering donated furniture. A local magazine couldn't help but notice the value of this partner's work to the community:

Movers and Shakers meets the physical needs of families in crisis thanks to the generosity of furniture donors and volunteers. Two Saturdays per month, all through the year, volunteers load up at 8 a.m. After making one or two deliveries, they meander through Gwinnett and North Fulton counties making prearranged pickups of donated furniture. These donations are then warehoused and inventoried for future deliveries.

The volunteers who drive trucks and move furniture love working with Movers and Shakers! It takes no advance preparation and requires no long-term commitment, but makes a significant difference and is very rewarding. As a side benefit, they have fun driving around in trucks and figuring out how best to load the assortment of furniture they pick up. Adult small groups, families, high school groups and dads and teens working together make up the volunteer pool.

Churches currently involved with the ministry include Peachtree Corners Baptist, Dunwoody Baptist, Victory World Church and Perimeter Church. Other churches are encouraged to join in. Movers and Shakers gives churches a simple outlet for service, a source of furniture for families in need and a unique service experience for small groups, youth groups and families.[4]

Because the World Is Sinking

We are witnessing the demise of a culture. Why are the issues of poverty, education, justice, and family increasingly heartbreaking?

Why does volunteering sometimes feel like cleaning a house that never gets clean? Why are the needs so pressing? Why did Unite! simply have to exist? Why are there so many who, in their despair over the news and the needs of the world around them, throw up their hands and admit defeat?

Because the world itself is sinking. The apostle Paul recognized it: "We know that the whole creation has been groaning as in the pains of childbirth right up to the present time. Not only so, but we ourselves, who have the firstfruits of the Spirit, groan inwardly as we wait eagerly for our adoption as sons, the redemption of our bodies" (Rom. 8:22–23 NIV). If you pay attention, you can hear the difference between groans of hopelessness and groans of hope. As we listen closely to the community, we can't help but hear cries of despair. Sure, we aren't immune to desperation ourselves. In fact, because as Christ-followers we anticipate something we haven't yet attained, we groan just like everyone else. But anticipation spells hope. As those who await the hope of heaven, we are called to live out that hope in a dying world, and as we do, the impact has dynamic possibilities. The gospel is, by its very nature, transformational. It begins with a life. It moves from life to life. And because it cannot be contained, it has the potential to transform entire communities.

The Community Outreach arm of Perimeter Church and Unite! are pursuing bigger goals than the creation of a network of organizations and volunteers. Yes, we have stories to tell of lives changed, but it doesn't stop there. The aim is community transformation. Perimeter Church expresses it this way:

- The people in our community, in ever-increasing numbers across ethnic and socioeconomic boundaries, are becoming members of Christ's body, the church, becoming passionately committed to him, and engaging in word and deed ministry.
- The believers' lifestyles are becoming increasingly marked by high moral standards. They are practicing indiscriminate love, demonstrating spiritual integrity in all their relationships, living by faith in Christ, attempting faith-oriented goals, and speaking the truth regardless of the consequences.

- Local churches are increasingly working together in the unity of the Spirit, as the body of Christ, ministering to the needs of the community, and working for justice for the powerless and reconciliation.
- The educational, judicial, political, business, and social structures in our community are beginning to reflect conformity with the Word of God.

This isn't a political platform. It isn't a wish list. It isn't an over-spiritualization with no real meaning. It is a pledge to be the church in all its vibrant, life-changing, world-shaking glory.

Because Drowning Happens Every Day

She was certain she was going to sink. And as sinking people often feel, she was certain she would drop out of sight, off the radar, into oblivion, all alone. Little did she know a human chain had already been rallied on her behalf. The links in that chain were already stretching across the frozen, broken, desperate terrain of her life, searching for women just like her. In that moment, when she was certain of death, they found her.

Listen to one woman's description of her own rescue:

I am the twenty-eight-year-old mother of three beautiful children. My life before coming to Rainbow Village was awful. I was with a man who abused me mentally, sexually, physically, and financially. He was also abusive to our two-year-old son. He was a very controlling man, so much so that I could not have a cell phone or a car. I left my husband while five months pregnant with twins. I was afraid and unsure of what the future held for me and my children. My son and I stayed in a domestic violence shelter in Fulton County for one and a half months. After the birth of my twins, I got a job and heard about Rainbow Village. I completed an application and went through the interview process with the case manager for Rainbow Village. You can imagine my relief when I was told I had been accepted into the program. Rainbow Village has become a safe haven for me and my children. They have taught me how to budget my money and how to manage a savings account, how to be responsible for myself and not be dependent on others, and most importantly they have given my family lots of love. They have even made our holidays special! Rainbow Village has taught me how to live on my own. I no longer have to depend on my parents, a man, or anyone else. Rainbow Village has become my family, and I thank them for everything!

Drill deeper into our partnerships with organizations like Rainbow Village—those on the front line who relish daring rescues—and you'll find that, while they are about the community, they have an equally important parallel focus. They are about people. Drowning people. Individuals who, one by one, need the strong hand at the end of a courageous human chain of compassion. People who, often in the process of being saved from whatever it is that holds them under, find the Savior.

Think about It

What is . . .

Who are the ministries and organizations that you are currently partnering with in your community?

How do you evaluate whom to partner with in your community?

Who Are We?

From the beginning the staff and leadership of our Community Outreach ministry at Perimeter Church determined to be facilitators rather than performers. In our first year as a functioning department with a daily employee presence at the church, we had to reeducate the rest of the staff at Perimeter. We were not a convenient catchall for every community need. We were not the go-to workforce for every pet project. Our mission was bigger than that.

Here's how it works: The link between us and our partners is our lay leaders. The lay leaders champion a particular partner to the church. That partner then offers opportunities for our people as well as the other churches to serve. Through Unite! more churches have become aware of needs and gotten involved with these partners. This kind of partnership has had an impact exponentially greater than any ministry our staff and church could expect to do by themselves.

Partnering vs. Power; Modern vs. Postmodern

Leadership looks a lot different these days, doesn't it? Matthew Kirdahy, a leadership reporter for Forbes.com, was asked if Mafioso boss Tony Soprano would make it in Wall Street today. The answer, unhesitatingly: no. That's because today's young businessmen and women value a horizontal leadership style rather than a vertical one. They work best within a network rather than a top-down chain of command. So where, if not in the crime family world, would a Tony Soprano find his niche as a leader? Perhaps in the military, suggests Kirdahy. The battlefield—where lives are literally on the line—is the only place in today's world where fear-inspired management is effective.[5]

The postmodern value of networking isn't limited to the boardrooms of Fortune 500 companies; it has permeated the church as well. Today's Christian innovators (it might be safe to say this entire generation of believers) are just as unlikely to respond to a "big boss" style of leadership in the church.

When Perimeter Church determined to partner with other churches and ministries, without realizing it we were following an emerging sociological trend. Partnering naturally diffused the authoritative management approach the church has employed for centuries. We don't share just resources with our partners; we share authority and all the responsibilities that go with it: decision making, equipping, and vision casting.

What could be . . .

It is five years down the road, and you and your church have a network of partnerships with ministries in your city:

- How did you develop relationships with these specific partners?
- What have you done to mobilize the people in your church to connect with these partners?
- What difficult decisions did you have to make and what obstacles did you have to overcome?

What will be . . .

What strategic steps can you take to develop partners in your community? If you already have partnerships, how can you refine your process?

What plans can you make to mobilize your people to get involved in your partner ministries?

What we did . . .

In the last chapter, I mentioned meeting with ministry and church leaders. These meetings became more and more focused over time. We held monthly pastors' luncheons in order to develop our friendships with other churches.

Early on, we decided to rely on lay leaders to keep our ministry partners connected to our people. Of course this means our staff did a good bit of recruiting and equipping, but it didn't take long for the culture of leadership development at Perimeter to produce innovative lay leaders who stepped up to champion particular ministries. (To get a feel for the significance of these lay leaders and volunteers, check out Perimeter's Community Outreach website [www.perimeter.org/communityoutreach] and Perimeter's Community Outreach blog [www.touchedbyservice.blogspot.com].)

Picture This

Make a mental connection between human beings and chains, and you will most likely picture a criminal in captivity, shuffling to his cell with both feet manacled together by heavy shackles. The ghost of Jacob Marley wore rusty chains in his afterlife both as penance and as a warning to his greedy partner, Ebenezer Scrooge. These clanking chains were no graceful adornment.

Bind several lengths of chains together into a fabric, and you have the means to produce a garment. And if you were a soldier in just about any army during the Dark Ages, you would have considered clothing formed of chains a godsend. Chainmail was invented by the Celts, probably before the fifth century. *Maille* is the French word derived from the Latin *macula*, meaning a "mesh of net." This flexible metal armor endured as a defense mainstay until the Middle Ages, when plate armor eventually edged it out of use altogether. But until then, chainmail was the cat's meow among military men worldwide.

And no wonder. Chainmail was fashioned by a master craftsman to protect the most vulnerable parts of a warrior's body. The coif, aventail, mail fringe, and bishop's mantle were designed specifically for the head. For the torso, the shirt, hauberk, skirt, and breeches.

For the upper limbs, mail sleeves and mittens, and for the lower limbs, chausses and sabatons.[6]

The classic chainmail shirt is a vivid picture of the power of partnership. It takes the image of a linear chain—one link added to another link and then to another in one long line—and changes it into three-dimensional functionality.

Like all other movements that link the church together in a flexible force of kingdom power, Unite! has embraced the original intention of Perimeter Church by blanketing the community with a garment of grace. Our partnerships have allowed us to act on behalf of the least and the lost. The links in an ever-widening chain of relationships have enabled us to advance the kingdom into the world.

> The ice cracked several times, but the rescuers did not bolt until they had pulled the almost unconscious Crawford to safety.
>
> "Saved by a Human Chain: Boys and Girls
> Joined Hands to Rescue a Lad from Drowning,"
> *New York Times*, December 25, 1906

> Friendship is essentially a partnership.
>
> Aristotle

> A cord of three strands is not quickly broken.
>
> Ecclesiastes 4:12 NIV

Long Beach:
The Church as a Catalyst

If You Care to Look

"Thousands Struggle in the Shadow of Affluence" proclaims the local news article. In a nation girthed with a comfortable middle class, this isn't what we expect to hear about one of our own cities. A class divide that separates the well-to-do from the impoverished doesn't exist here, does it? That kind of gap is indigenous to third-world countries, not superpower nations, right? Or if we do discover it here, it's in our teeming urban areas or in the backwaters of the deep South. Surely it's not in the fifth largest city in sunny California.

Long Beach: where the very poor and the very wealthy coexist, but separately. The divorce of one class from the other is painful; the rift is wide. Long Beach: where 19 percent of the population lives below the national poverty line (less than $20,000 per year for a family of four), and 28 percent of the children live in poverty. Long Beach: ranked sixth in the nation for the concentration of its poor in seventeen downtrodden neighborhoods. The article continues:

> Take a walk in Long Beach and what do you see?
> Stray from the palm-lined streets by the ocean shore, the bustling hubs at Pine Avenue, the Pike or Belmont Shore; leave the manicured lawns of the Virginia Country Club area or the Bixby neighborhoods, and there's another Long Beach.

It is the Long Beach that struggles daily to make the rent, rather than the one that plops down a fortune for an ocean-view condo.

It is the Long Beach that relies on food stamps, free school breakfast and lunch programs and charity groups' grocery giveaways, not the one that dines on lower Pine Avenue.[7]

The complete title of the *Long Beach Press-Telegram* article, one of many about the condition of its city's poor is, "Thousands Struggle in the Shadow of Affluence: The Signs of Poverty Are Everywhere in Long Beach, If You Care to Look."

If you care to look. If the city of Long Beach could be personified as one human being, the wounded man languishing in a ditch in Jesus's parable of the Good Samaritan might describe him best. Long Beach, the downtrodden and beaten. Long Beach, the broken. Long Beach, the ignored and skirted around.

It is so much easier not to look.

That's because looking eventually calls for responsibility. And when looking leads to action, things get stirred up. The Samaritan looked, and his bank account took a hit. The others didn't even look, and, for them, everything stayed the same. Want to hold on to the status quo? Don't look.

Stirred to Action

In this decaying California city, Grace Brethren Church of Long Beach cared to look. They were compelled by the gospel to look, and when they did, they were stirred to action. Distill that action into one sentence and you have their passion: Our mission is to help followers of Jesus pursue the flourishing of Long Beach.[8] Out of this passion, Hope for Long Beach was founded with a clear directive to be the hands and feet of Jesus in relation to the poverty and need of their city. The leaders of HFLB answer the "why we do what we do" question this way:

Jesus came to this earth with a mission to put us into right relationship with God, others, and the world, and thus bring about the spiritual, social, and cultural flourishing of all creation. He invites us to join him in this mission.[9]

95

Hope for Long Beach is an example of the church catalyzing a movement in the city. HFLB is staffed and resourced heavily by Grace Brethren, but it isn't owned solely by them. It is a movement. A catalyst for change. And what a change it is making.

Susan Beeney, a member at Grace Brethren, cared to look at the grief-stricken of Long Beach. She observed that, in 2005, there were approximately thirty-five hundred deaths reported to the Long Beach Health Department. "When you do the math, that's over forty thousand people in Long Beach who are walking around, all ages, grieving the loss of someone they love and not knowing where to go."[10] She eventually founded New Hope Grief Support. In one year, with the help of a board and over one hundred volunteers, they held twenty-nine weekly grief groups, in which trained facilitators led support sessions for adults, teens, and children. And over the last three years, New Hope has also partnered with organizations nationwide to assist families of the military.

HFLB acts as a catalyst for a city movement that experiences and distributes common grace. Their strategy, outlined in more detail on their website, is to display this grace throughout society by working with nonprofit organizations, associations, schools, businesses, and government agencies:

- Create space for connections. Few places exist where leaders can build relationships without being asked to join a project or program. We build sandboxes for Christian leaders where they learn to play together.
- Train church leaders in the greater Long Beach area. We consult with churches individually, host an externally focused roundtable, and lead an annual day of service that encourages churches to look outside the walls of their congregation.
- Join/build collaborations around common causes. In addition to our work with nonprofit partners, we work with convening/training organizations such as Kingdom Causes and the Long Beach Nonprofit Partnership.
- Support entrepreneurs. From church planters to creative new nonprofits, we value the myriad expressions of mission manifested by followers of Jesus in Long Beach.

When a church cares to look at the city clamoring for care and attention right outside its own back door, it's amazing what can happen. When a church releases its resources of time and people and funding not just to meet needs but to take a city from floundering to flourishing, that's a veritable chemical reaction.

> Luckily, a priest was on his way down the same road, but when he saw him he angled across to the other side. Then a Levite religious man showed up; he also avoided the injured man. A Samaritan traveling the road came on him. When he saw the man's condition, his heart went out to him.
>
> Luke 10:31–33 Message

I'll be frank with my opinion. The larger world is not picking up the signals of compassion from the branch of Christianity of which I am a part. While Nicholas Kristof of the *New York Times* often applauds our movement for its far-flung programs in AIDS, home building, hospitals, and disaster response, we are not known as compassionate people as we do these things. All our good efforts are covered by the sense that we are proud, angry, and vindictive in our selective approaches to those needing some form of redemption. I don't want to be perceived as a hard person with an accusatory message who occasionally does good deeds. Much better to be perceived as the wounded healer who exchanges his bandages with the one who has none to offer back.

> Gordon MacDonald, editor at large of *Leadership*
> magazine and chair of World Relief

7

Transformation

It Works Both Ways

She just wanted to check her good deed off the list. Get it out of the way. Feel good about herself—that's what volunteerism is, right?—and move on. But it didn't work out quite that way. It almost never does.

Debra Potter chose the gig at a juvenile detention center for her Compassion in Action Weekend commitment because, she now admits, it was the shortest project on the list. She'd be home in time for lunch. It was 2004, and Debra was a new Christ-follower *and* a new staff member at Perimeter Church. As a fresh believer, she had a hunch serving was important. As a staff member, she felt the tug of obligation.

All was going as planned until a young girl sat next to Debra and poured out her story, her gut-wrenching story. Both victim and offender all rolled into one, the girl touched Debra's heart, and then, just as the volunteers were walking out the door, the girl touched her arm: "You're coming back next week, right?"

Next week turned into four years. Debra became one of many from seventeen churches who filed past the razor-wire gate each Saturday to worship and pray and learn and laugh with kids whose young lives were caught in a tragic interruption. Debra quickly learned the urgency of her role. Most of the kids were en route to somewhere else—wilderness camps, other detention centers, court-appointed foster care—so the volunteers had a small interval of time in which to make a connection, to impact lives for the kingdom.

Transformed Lives Transform Lives

The links in the chain that Community Outreach and Unite! use to connect with the world outside their doors are human ones. Yes, we extend our dollars, our resources, and our expertise, but we extend our people as well. God uses people to change the lives of other people. We wanted to make sure our people were themselves changed, altered into Christ's character, renovated into his likeness. Our commitment as a church to life-on-life missional discipleship was a good foundation, but we didn't want to take anything for granted. We wanted to deploy people who were ready, equipped, *transformed*.

We developed a seven-week training program on mercy and justice ministry for our Community Outreach lay leaders. These hour-long training sessions took place on Sunday mornings. Initially, this was the most important training and equipping we did. We made sure our instruction in the "how" of ministry included the heart. We did not want our people to do more damage than good when they served in the community. *How* we go is as important as going itself. If we are not personally, intimately changed to the core, we cannot hope to make change in the community.

Our agenda has evolved over time, but the basic elements of our training are:

1. mercy and justice mandate
2. motivation for mercy and justice
3. sharing the burden
4. blessed to be a blessing
5. prayer
6. cultural sensitivity
7. counting the cost[1]

We primarily used *Ministries of Mercy* by Tim Keller as a text.[2] Eventually we began to write our own material for this training. Our teaching is related to our hearts, our mind-set, and our worldview, no matter where we serve in the community. Because of that, it has served us well as an all-purpose piece. We have also helped write the mission section in our church discipleship curriculum, which focuses on word and deed mission. This vital portion of training challenges our people to deploy where they are called in the community and around the world. In our wealthy congregation, it has been important to emphasize that we are no different from those we serve and that we must enter into relationships with humility. It is not about fixing people; it is about building reciprocal relationships. Our church was committed to avoiding the "knight in shining armor" model. We wanted our people committed to building relationships, not mounting rescue missions.

Our partners also offer their own training depending on how a person is serving with them. This material is much more specific to the volunteer position and also related to the ministry and organization and their unique focus. Equipping is yet another way we communicate respect to our partners. We aren't the final word on preparation for ministry. When it comes to our partners, we bow to their expertise by allowing them the privilege of stepping into the coach/instructor role. In fact, while our Community Outreach lay leaders go through Perimeter's seven-week training, most volunteers do not. Because we equip our leaders well and choose our partners with care, we can entrust volunteers to them and rest assured they will be adequately prepared for the work.

Transforming Lives Transforms Lives

Our goal has always been community transformation; we did not anticipate how much *we* would be transformed in the process. But it makes sense. We wanted to be a church of influence, not a successful church, and influence has a way of rebounding on the influencer. Influence makes a difference in both directions: The influencer almost always ends up joining the ranks of the influenced. As the stories of personal transformation began to roll in, we knew we needed to chronicle them. "Touched by Service," a blog dedicated to telling these stories, is full of testimonies like these:

> I've been there preaching or conducting a Bible study when all of a sudden one of the men will stand up, hold his hands in the air, and tell me he wants to be saved. Other inmates who are Christians and I will lay hands on that one man and pray over him; we've even baptized men in there. I get to see God move among us. All these years later, even though we went there to serve the prisoners, when we are leaving the prison one or more of us will say, "It feels like it was me who was blessed tonight." We agree that is the reward for exercising the gifts God gave us.
>
> Jim, Prison Ministry[3]

> I'm sure the greatest reward for a volunteer is the opportunity to tangibly experience God's love through the care they are providing the refugees. I think all volunteers begin their interaction with the refugees believing they are giving something to the refugee families, and they are. But after a while, as the volunteers get to know the families and understand their unique story, the volunteers begin to realize they are a part of God's provision for the refugees. It becomes a testimony of God's desire and ability to provide for all of us. It is wonderful to realize we serve a God who does that. Although most of us will never experience the conditions the refugees have experienced, it is reassuring to us that should we face such adversity, God will be there for us too.
>
> Joshua, World Relief[4]

> The cycle of blessing means a young girl saw God's plan . . . as messy and tiring as it was, to receive the blessings he had been waiting to pour on her. . . . The cycle continued in the lives of the family who took her in. . . . And then there was God's blessing to us—the opportunity for our own teen foster girls to see a success story, a girl who came out of foster care happy and strong.
>
> Jeanne, Promise686[5]

Debra Potter jumped into what she considered a little pool of do-goodism and discovered a vast ocean of God's plan to transform not just the community but her own life. She was swept away by the beauty of God's heart responding through God's people in the community. Spend just a few moments with Debra today and you may feel the same tug. Her passion is that compelling.

Debra is now the director of Community Outreach at Perimeter Church. She mobilizes Perimeter people to get involved with our partner ministries. That means she sees both sides of the transformation miracle. She hears the reverberating sound of influence as it echoes from both the influenced and the influencers. And she is enamored with the sound. Like so many others, while going about the kingdom work of transformation, *she* was transformed.

Think about It

What is . . .

Is there a Debra Potter in your church? If so, does she (or he) have an outlet for becoming a part of your community's transformation? Where can she plug in and, in the process, be transformed herself?

How do you equip the people in your church to serve in the community? Is there anything you haven't attempted yet because you aren't yet equipped?

What could be . . .

Make a list of the qualities that would exist in the lives of the people in your church if they, by transforming the community through service, were themselves transformed. Consider the ripple effect of this kind of change over the next five years.

What will be . . .

What are a few steps you can begin taking now to mobilize your people outside the four walls of your church?

What can you begin doing now to equip them?

What means can you use to capture the stories that will result?

What we did . . .

We equipped our Community Outreach leaders with a seven-week training that focused on heart issues and dealt with the "knight in shining armor" mentality.

We also began planning our first Compassion in Action Weekend. Although I will address it later on, now is a good place to mention that important event. The first weekend took us a long way down the road of community transformation for several reasons:

- It immediately invested our small band of staff, volunteers, churches, and ministries into something much bigger than we were.
- It gave us a project for the churches and ministries who came on board to rally around.
- It provided a one-weekend venue to introduce volunteers to ministries.
- As in Debra's experience, it gave those ministries faces.
- Actually doing something in the community created more passion for ministry among our people than any sermon or seminar could.

Picture This

The Romans, famous for their roads, thought of it first. Their roads marked their conquests, so why not mark the roads? They first erected stone obelisks—milestones (from the Latin *milliarium*)—at intervals of roughly one mile along Appian Way. They later marked the Roman roads that reached into Western Europe. These milestones gave travelers predictable markers for their progress in their journeys. We now use the term *milestone* to denote significant moments in the figurative journey of life.

Picture a moss-covered slab of granite sinking in the grass near a country road in Wales, and you may imagine a lonely traveler or a solitary sheepherder passing by. But the Romans built their milestones primarily for their troops, as an ancient GPS for a band of travelers.

Consider the noteworthy milestones in "The History of You." In your travels through life, you probably arrived at those most meaningful markers, those pivotal junctures, in the company of others. On the road of life, we rarely reach our milestones alone. We follow others or we take them with us. You got your degree, you married your spouse, you began your first job, you had your first child, you made strides in an important relationship, or you made big decisions. These milestones mark not only your personal history but also the people who influenced you and the people you influenced along the way. Adulthood, career, marriage, friendship, and parenthood are all milestones with the potential to transform your life and the lives of those who traveled with you there.

Keep it simple; you are the equipment.

Luke 9:3 Message

You must begin with your own life-giving lives. It's who you are, not what you say and do, that counts. Your true being brims over into true words and deeds.

Luke 6:45 Message

The star in this drama, to whom I'm a mere stagehand, will change your life. I'm baptizing you here in the river, turning your old life in for a kingdom life. His baptism—a holy baptism by the Holy Spirit—will change you from the inside out.

John the Baptist, speaking of Jesus (Mark 1:7–8 Message)

You don't choose your family. They are God's gift to you, as you are to them.

Desmond Tutu

It's not only children who grow. Parents do too.

Joyce Maynard, author of young
adult literature and professor at
Sarah Lawrence College

Little Rock:
New Paradigms in Structure

A Flagship Church Leads the Way

When you hear the words "You remind me of . . ." how do you react? Depends on who it is you're being compared to, right? A comparison can be a compliment or an insult. It can confirm the best in you or highlight the worst.

In my conversations with leaders of community outreach in cities, I found a comparison between Perimeter Church in Atlanta and Fellowship Bible in Little Rock that I didn't find with any other church. And that was a compliment. The groundbreaking work of community transformation in Little Rock, Arkansas, is something we intentionally emulated from the beginning. You could say we're drafting in their wake. We don't mind being compared to them, not at all.

In particular, we share one vital uniqueness. Unlike similar initiatives in other cities, we are both large flagship churches giving servant leadership to city transformation movements. Often the "powerful" megachurches in the megacities don't collaborate with other churches. They don't need to. They are fully capable of launching a successful ministry by themselves. But we became convinced, as did Fellowship Bible before us, that the needs were big enough to require the influence of both big and small churches. If you're talk-

106

ing need, there's certainly enough to go around. Why not unite as one to meet those needs head-on?

Often the barriers to effectively tackling issues in any city center are lack of funding and lack of staffing. That's where the flagship churches can come to the rescue. If more of us would offer our resources of staff and budget, we could get the job done together.

Fellowship Bible showed us the way. When we saw how freely and humbly they gave their resources—not demanding power because they were the "big dog"—we decided we wanted to be like them when we grew up. We wanted to fill in the gaps—that's primarily funding and staffing—without taking the credit. We wanted to share the passion for community transformation with as many churches and partners as we could, because we could. That's simply stewardship.

Refusing to Fly Its Own Flag

Another pattern we learned from Little Rock is the need to narrow the spotlight of our ministry. Actually, this is now becoming accepted wisdom among leaders who are committed to community outreach. The Nehemiah Group, a network of pastors and ministry leaders in Little Rock, has Area Pastors' Leadership Communities divided by geography.[6] Mission Houston, a nonprofit that works with area churches toward the goal of spiritual and social transformation in greater Houston, has divided their city into forty-five Community Study Areas for people to work together.[7] These examples and others confirmed our decision to limit the focus of Community Outreach to the twelve-mile radius around Perimeter Church and to let Unite! grow by regions around metro Atlanta. Historically, attempting to meet the vast needs of the city without addressing them segment by segment has been a lesson in futility. Breaking them down to bite-sized pieces is the only way to digest the sprawling problems in our cities.

For over ten years, Fellowship Bible has hosted a community outreach event called Sharefest, the event we modeled our Compassion in Action Weekends around. If you troll around on the Sharefest website (www.sharefest.org), you can't help but notice a few things. First, it's just about impossible to figure out who's in charge. That's because the input from Fellowship Bible isn't any more or less valuable than the input from the other churches involved. It is and has always been a "freewill offering," no strings attached. Sharefest, like Unite!, is a movement, not an organization or a parachurch ministry. Second, you'll note that the training resources are incredibly flexible. Small churches and their unique gifts and abilities are taken into account. And you'll find a list of other cities where Sharefest-type events are held. Around twenty of them are listed, some with the same name, but that is only a sampling. Forty to fifty cities in the United States and at least two in other countries hold these events. Clearly, Fellowship Bible was a catalyst of something big, but they don't have a proprietary hold on their ideas. From start to finish, this is kingdom business, and in kingdom business everything—*everything*—belongs to the King.

Fellowship Bible Church is a flagship that refuses to fly its own flag. After decades of church-growth strategies that seem to be nothing but sophisticated marketing schemes for the local church, this approach is refreshing. It takes the pressure off. If our job is to advance the kingdom instead of growing our churches or our programs, we can all breathe a sigh of relief . . . and get to work.

I planted the seed, Apollos watered it, but God made it grow.

1 Corinthians 3:6 NIV

In our many years of serving our respective communities, we can think of no single effort that even approaches Sharefest in impact on our two cities.

Mayor Jim Dailey, Little Rock, Arkansas, and Mayor Patrick Hays, North Little Rock, Arkansas

8

Unity

But First We Experienced a Split

Does anyone remember when the word *ecumenical* was cutting-edge, almost to the point of scandalous? When was that? A mere genera-tion ago? The sheer suggestion that denominations could overlap each others' territory was nigh unto impossible as recently as the 1970s. "Imagine worshiping with the Presbyterians!" exclaimed the Baptists. "Surely we can't rub shoulders with those Methodists?" said the Pentecostals. Even those close-to-kin pairings—the Lutherans and the Episcopalians or the AME and the Southern Baptists—kept within the invisible boundaries created by history, tradition, and theology.

And then it all began to change. Nondenominational churches helped usher in a new age of label-lessness. Churches became less homogeneous, at least where denomination was concerned, and more like devout melting pots. It was a step in the right direction.

But are we unified now? Are we really there yet? Is there a sense—a reality so strong that onlookers can actually observe it—that we are all particles in the same nucleus, no matter how far apart we might be in geography, culture, background, race, personal preferences, and, yes, even the nuances of our theology? Is it more than just lip service that we are "many parts, but one body" (1 Cor. 12:20 NIV)? Or have we simply replaced those old disunities with new ones? Big vs. small. Cool vs. traditional. Charismatic vs. liturgical. Conservative vs. liberal. Politically active vs. complacent. Public school vs. private. *Any* school vs. homeschool. Drinkers vs. teetotalers. The list could go on ad infinitum.

The truth is the church has a track record of disunity about as long and evolved as its history. In the educated opinion of many, one of the biggest barriers to the message of the gospel—ranking right up there with the cosmic questions of suffering and the origin of evil—is our lack of unity. Like a doctor examining an X-ray film, the world has held up its pictures of the church to the light for centuries. The world has looked closely and detected our hairline fractures and our compound breaks, and the diagnosis is often dead-on. "That's not really *us*," we protest. But it's really hard to deny the massive ruptures in Northern Ireland or the shattering shame of the Dark Ages. It is even more difficult to deny the more than thirty-eight thousand Christian denominations in existence today.[1] In fact, our disunity may well be a major reason for the existence of apologetics. If we could just get along, maybe the world wouldn't be quite so skeptical.

Creating Unity

So how do we preach the gospel—the ultimate call to unity—when we aren't what we preach? When our methods vary enough to be contradictory? When our differences don't just confuse the world but distract us from our purpose? When even the petty things threaten to split us apart? When decisions about carpet color and bulletin inserts and music styles keep us from addressing the bigger issues?

When Perimeter Church set out to become a church of influence, we weren't necessarily thinking about unity; that particular issue wasn't our bull's-eye. But it is what we *weren't* thinking about that bolstered authentic unity. We weren't thinking about Perimeter Church. We made a deliberate shift in our focus from our building, our programs, our capital campaigns, our reputation, and our staff to the least and the lost in our community. Thus, without being particularly intentional about it, the message of unity and the method of creating it became one and the same.

In their book *To Transform a City*, Eric Swanson and Sam Williams spell it out a bit more intentionally:

> Unity is a means, not an end, which explains the failure of most ecumenical movements. If unity is our main goal, we will never get there. Phil Butler in a paper entitled, "15 Key Principles for Success in Kingdom Collaboration," writes, "Successful networks/partnerships develop in order to accomplish a specific vision or task. Cooperation for cooperation's sake is a sure recipe for failure. Warm 'fellowship' is not enough. This means lasting cooperation focuses primarily on what (objectives) rather than how (structure). Form always follows function—not the other way around. Consensus is usually better than constitution! Focus on purpose. Structure should only be the minimum required to get the job done."
>
> God's intention is that we be unified through a shared mission—helping people understand through word and deed, that Jesus is sent from God and that he loves every person on earth as much as he loves his own son Jesus.[2]

Can we really hope to defeat disunity? Can our ugliest flaw as a church worldwide—sibling rivalry—suffer a fatal blow? Perhaps it can if we turn our attention to the kingdom and away from the church. If we care more about the advancement of the realm of Christ's reign than the advancement of our own organizations. If we hold kingdom expansion as a higher value than growing the local church.

This is what Jesus has had in mind all along. Unity has been on his heart for us from the beginning:

> In the same way that you gave me a mission in the world, I give them a mission in the world. I'm consecrating myself for their sakes so they'll be truth-consecrated in their mission. I'm praying not only for them but also for those who will believe in me because of them and their witness about me. The goal is for all of them to become one heart and mind—just as you, Father, are in me and I in you, so they might be one heart and mind with us. Then the world might believe that you, in fact, sent me. The same glory you gave me, I gave them,

Which Gospel Is It?

In 1910, Presbyterians proclaimed:

"The great ends of the church are the proclamation of the gospel for the salvation of humankind; the shelter, nurture, and spiritual fellowship of the children of God; the maintenance of divine worship; the preservation of truth; the promotion of social righteousness; and the exhibition of the Kingdom of Heaven to the world."[3]

That statement beautifully blends both the gospel of salvation and the social gospel—a trend that developed in the church in the United States in the nineteenth century in reaction to the poverty and injustice of post–Civil War times and continued until the civil rights movement.

While caring for the needs of the least and the lost does indeed exhibit "the Kingdom of Heaven to the world," the social gospel, instigated some say by Charles Sheldon and his book *In His Steps*, was not without critics within the church. It may be that conservative Christians were skeptical for good reason: "That movement, championed chiefly by mainline Protestant theologians, linked social ministry to liberal theology that questioned biblical authority."[4]

Evangelical Christians, in their zeal to preserve the Word spoken, often threw out the baby with the bathwater. They rejected actions and preferred words. In doing so, the church became irrelevant to our culture.

so they'll be as unified and together as we are—I in them and you in me. Then they'll be mature in this oneness, and give the godless world evidence that you've sent me and loved them in the same way you've loved me.

John 17:18–23 Message

A Double Whammy

As we began to establish a community outreach ministry at Perimeter, it wasn't long before two profound truths rose to the surface:

1. We were commissioned to give the church away. If we, the local church, decreased and the kingdom increased, it didn't matter. That's because the kingdom mattered more.
2. We had to do ministry in the context of partnership. We couldn't do it alone.

These two truths meant nothing unless we acted on them. They were the two truths that drove our mission. They were the two truths that unified us. And those two truths led to a split.

How's that?

Yes, it's true. We experienced a split . . . a powerful one. But before describing the disunity we actually brought on ourselves, let's examine the unity we experienced as we began to give ourselves away.

An atom is the fundamental building block of all matter. You remember that from high school chemistry. Over one hundred elements, or varieties of atoms, exist on the periodic table. The hydrogen atom is the smallest, with a diameter of 10^{-8} cm. You probably also remember that atoms have neutrons, protons, and electrons, with a lot of empty space in between—microscopic empty space.

When atoms join together, they form compounds. Atoms bond by sharing electrons, the particles that swirl around the nucleus. When atoms bond to form a compound, the nuclei of each atom remains the same. This is called a chemical reaction; it happens under normal conditions and requires a normal exertion of energy. Bonding in this way transforms the atoms involved. They will never be the same.

Then there's nuclear fusion. That's when atoms fuse together at the core, the nucleus. And they don't fuse under normal circumstances. Fusion requires massive amounts of energy—in the form of heat—to occur. Scientists are still researching ways to harness fusion as a source of energy. As volatile and unique as nuclear fusion is, it does happen naturally all the time. In the crucible of space, where a high density and temperature environment exists, stars glow with a nuclear energy more intense than anything we experience here on earth.[5]

When we made the pivotal decision to bond with outside ministry partners to become a church of influence in our community, we created a "unity reaction." When we decided to extend that bond to other churches, the reaction became powerful. It exploded. And when it exploded it began to give off light.

But there's another nuclear reaction even more powerful than fusion: nuclear fission. When an atom is split, a neutron is released and a chain reaction begins. Unfortunately, the pictures that spring to mind with any mention of splitting atoms are mushroom clouds over Hiroshima or the fallout of Chernobyl. Dangerous? Yes, in some instances, but nuclear fission provides power without emit-

Losing Our Marbles

Imagine two hundred marbles lying in a vaguely circular pattern on a flat surface. What would happen if someone took just one marble and threw it at all the others? They would fly out in all directions, wouldn't they? The circle would widen considerably.[6]

That's the effect of nuclear fission, of splitting the atom. It isn't safe or predictable or orderly. But it produces expansion. The possibilities seem nearly limitless when this kind of shake-up occurs.

ting harmful pollutants into our atmosphere. It is our second largest energy source after coal. Splitting the atom is a powerful reaction we rely on to live.

To flesh out our ministry in the community, we knew we had to split the atom. Unite! became its own initiative, and it has never been a ministry of Perimeter Church. The movement that is Unite! grew out of a realization that one church with a community outreach ministry could not make a big enough kingdom impact. Community Outreach essentially serves our church by propelling it into ministry. Unite! serves the community by propelling *churches* to meet its needs. The two, though formed from the same "atom," are really quite different:

- Community Outreach: connecting the people of Perimeter Church with ministry partners and deploying them into the community. You might consider this the implosion impact, the reaction that reached into our church and turned our hearts inside out for the least and the lost. This is a separately staffed, funded, and functioning department of Perimeter Church.
- Unite!: deploying the church at large—local churches—into the community. Unite! is the consortium of kingdom-minded churches that grew out of a desire among more than one church to make a bigger difference in our city. It isn't a department of one church; it isn't a parachurch ministry. It is a movement; it is an organism instead of an organization.

Unite!

Both initiatives embrace kingdom values, but Unite! has become something less familiar looking to the average church staff member or volunteer than Community Outreach. That's because it operates *among* churches, not *in* them. This unique approach requires a careful communication of values. For example, with our focus on "good deeds," the perception crops up from time to time that we are not about the verbal gospel. Not so. We are not the United Way; we are a group of biblically based churches. Such confusion necessitates a clear outline of our values:

1. Dependence upon God as our source. We believe only God can change hearts. Our desire is to create avenues for people from various churches to pray together. Therefore, we are facilitating a prayer movement in our community and city as an integral part of Unite!
2. The local church. We believe the local church is the primary vehicle for the expansion of God's kingdom. As we minister to people, our goal ultimately is to connect them with a local church.
3. Holistic ministry. We believe in a scriptural mandate to share the gospel as well as to live it out by meeting the needs of others. Both word and deed are the means to building the kingdom.
4. Collaboration. We believe the most effective means of making a kingdom impact in Atlanta is within the context of relationships between churches and organizations in the public and private sector.

Getting Churches Started

When a church plans to participate in Unite!'s Compassion in Action Weekend, we give them a church starter packet that includes, among other things, these guidelines:

1. Develop a plan for your congregation's involvement.
2. Consider partnering with another church in your service projects.
3. Recruit a Compassion in Action coordinator for your congregation.
4. Choose service projects for your congregation.
5. Cast a vision of Compassion in Action and projects to your congregation.
6. Recruit service project leaders to oversee service projects.
7. Post service projects online by September 1.
8. Invite volunteers to sign up for service projects.
9. Cast a vision for volunteers to continue serving throughout the year.

Concerted kingdom thinking may well be the first step toward unity in today's body of Christ. To a decidedly unconvinced world, unity says it all. The linchpin of Unite! and Community Outreach is kingdom priority. It doesn't matter if no quantifiable gain comes back to our church. It doesn't matter who gets the credit or enjoys the benefits. In our chosen context, these things don't matter. We have decided to make the kingdom matter more.

The challenge to the church today is this: Will we make kingdom work our priority? Will we pursue God's heart for the world? Will we become the hands and feet of Jesus outside the walls of our churches? And will we do all of these things whether they grow our local body or not? If we do, we may accomplish a miraculous feat without even trying: We may unify the body of Christ. If we do *that*, the onlooking world may well sit up and take notice.

Think about It

What is . . .

Can you list some examples of ways your church is focused on the broader kingdom and not just on your church and its ministries? What are the ways you are giving yourselves away as a church?

What could be . . .

Partnering with other churches is a huge step toward unity. Let's say you began partnering with area churches five years ago:

- What were the critical factors that led to this partnering among the churches?
- What were the greatest obstacles to overcome?
- What were the early indicators that your efforts were heading in the right direction?

What will be . . .

Make a list of like-minded churches and plan a meeting of pastors and key leaders to pray about the needs of your city.

What is one thing you can do during the next six months to move toward working together with these churches for the transformation of your city?

What we did . . .

We formed Unite! as a prayerfully orchestrated split from Perimeter's Community Outreach department.

In addition to identifying me as the overall leader, or director, to give leadership to Unite!, we formed an overall leadership team made up of representatives from eight churches. This team was (and still is) very diverse ethnically, culturally, and denominationally. Here is a brief overview of how this team functions:

- The team developed both vision and mission statements and strategic impact areas.
- The team meets monthly to plan, to continue the overall vision, and to chart progress.
- We have developed a central means of distributing communications (see www.UniteUs.org).
- We host monthly Unite! luncheons for the purpose of casting vision, networking, and sharing about needs in the community. The team focuses on ongoing initiatives much more than one-time events.

Picture This

Long before 1944, when Otto Hahn discovered nuclear fission, a community of thinkers had begun the study of how matter behaves. Before nuclear fission was even a remote consideration, the world would see a chain reaction of discoveries: J. J. Thomson isolated the electron in 1898. Arthur Holly Compton of the United States later won the Nobel Prize for his discoveries about electrons and X-ray technology. Ideas about the atom were further defined by Ernest Rutherford. Working with Rutherford was a young Danish physicist named Niels Bohr, who won the Nobel Prize in 1922 for his part in their work. By 1939, Bohr and others began to ask the question, What happens to a uranium atom when a neutron hits it? Bohr recognized that he did not make his discoveries in a vacuum:

> If, twenty-five years ago, I had the good fortune to give a modest contribution to this development, it was, above all, thanks to the hospitality I then, as a young man, enjoyed in the famous laboratories of England. In particular, I think with grateful emotion of the unique friendliness and straightforwardness with which Rutherford, in the midst of his unceasing creative activity, was always prepared to listen to any student behind whose youthful inexperience he perceived a serious interest.[7]

Bohr's collaborators were both past and present—those who preceded him in research and those in the international community who worked alongside him.

No doubt about it, powerful things happen when the church collaborates, when we reach back and build on the work others did before us and when we reach forward to continue the work—when we seek his kingdom first . . . together.

> Giving thanks to the Father, who has qualified you to share in the inheritance of the saints in the kingdom of light. For he has rescued us from the dominion of darkness and brought us into the kingdom of the Son he loves, in whom we have redemption, the forgiveness of sins.
>
> Colossians 1:12–14 NIV

9

We Have Liftoff

The First Compassion in Action Weekend

R-7 Semyorka (which in Russian simply means "the digit seven"), Titan II, Atlas, Saturn V. The names sound vaguely familiar, don't they? Saturn V probably gives it away. Yes, these terms have something to do with space travel. And, no, unless you are a NASA fanatic, you wouldn't consider them household words. They fall into a more obscure category, one you might encounter in "Final Jeopardy."

They aren't the rock stars of space flight, but these babies sure played a major role. They were solid booster rockets—the unsung, unmanned heroes of the Soviet Union and NASA. Each one paired with a more well-known shuttle or satellite to launch it into the atmosphere and out into space. In 1957, Sputnik became the first earth-orbiting satellite with the help of R-7 Semyorka, the first carrier rocket. In the United States, Atlas was used to launch most of the Mercury manned satellites, Titan II for Gemini, and Saturn V for Apollo.[1]

The very existence of booster rockets illustrates a simple truth: For something to take flight, it needs a propellant, and if that thing is really going to fly, the propellant must be delivered in a safe and effective way. From launchpad to the stars, a key element in space exploration has always been the booster rocket.

It sounds simple, but it isn't. For decades, the R-7 rocket model was the most-used means of launching satellites worldwide, but not every launch was successful. The first two of four tests failed before Sputnik catapulted into the sky on October 4, 1957. The logs of later attempts at flight are peppered with almost as many failures as successes. The cryptic remarks "exploded," "guidance system malfunction," and "disintegrated" fill the historical record of space exploration.

And so another simple truth can be found in the history of space travel: Launching things is difficult and dangerous. Prepare for failures to mingle with successes. But when success happens, when it actually works and the thing is lofted into the heavens and soars, prepare to be awed.

Countdown to Launch

It was early in 2003. Community Outreach was a newly functioning entity at Perimeter Church. The relationships that were to form Unite! were building momentum. Our goal: community transformation. Our plan: to turn our hearts inside out for the least and the lost. We weren't just dreaming it; we were doing it. Yet the dream was big—so big we knew it needed a powerful booster rocket to get it off the ground and up into the air.

In the planning stages, our "lab" became conversations with other pastors and leaders, specifically the staff at Hopewell Missionary Baptist Church. Inspired by Fellowship Bible's Sharefest in Little Rock and stirred by our discussions about church partnership, we began to gather fuel for the next step: a weekend event. Perimeter and Hopewell were committed to doing the work of community transformation in an under-the-radar way, but we couldn't help but imagine what might happen if we gathered more churches and unleashed them into the neighborhood on one weekend. Surely such a gathering could be the boost we needed to get our people into the community. We weren't the only ones thinking that way. By the time our first Compassion in Action Weekend took place in the fall of 2003, thirty churches had joined us. We were ready for takeoff!

The Compassion in Action Weekend did indeed propel our people and area churches into wider kingdom work in our community, but the rich fuel that swirled on the launchpad wasn't the event but the relationships.

Fueling the Launch

Early in my ministry as a youth pastor, I discovered the perils of my own competitive nature: I came dangerously close to burning out. It is all too easy to compare myself with others as if we are side by side in a race. But fellow ministers are not competitors; they are teammates. That early brush with disaster was averted because I had a relationship with a mentor who loved me through it. Since then I've discovered that doing ministry *in synergy* is more effective and healthy than doing it in competition with others. If I can build relationships with like-minded people, we can—together—accomplish far greater goals in a far greater way.

And ministry can be lonely. We need each other. We need support, encouragement, and accountability; we need relationships. They are the key to sustainability in any kingdom endeavor. As we began formulating the foundation of Unite!, we determined to make relationships our cornerstone. If we wanted to stay in the game for the long haul, our friendships would have to be integral every step along the way.

As we launched Community Outreach, I began building relationships with missions pastors and other staff for this very reason. I gathered together a group of local missions staff members from other churches for monthly meetings. The primary purpose was to build friendships with one another and to encourage one another through prayer. At these meetings, we each shared about our personal lives, our churches, and our ministries. We prayed for one another, and we learned from one another. This was vital in laying the foundation for Unite! This was our primary fuel. It was in this context of friendship that we planned the first Compassion in Action Weekend, and it sustains the movement today.

In addition to these gatherings, I also started going to several meetings of pastors and leaders taking place in our area. In a number of local communities, pastors met together regularly. I showed up at one such meeting in March of 2003 and found the turnout disappointingly small. Two of us from Perimeter, two from Hopewell Missionary Baptist, and a few others attended this meeting. Hopewell Missionary Baptist is one of the large African-American churches in Atlanta. It is only fifteen minutes from our church. At the time, we had no significant relationship with this church, but we knew of each other. Because of the small turnout at the lunch, we were able to discuss why so few wanted to meet for relationship and to work together. At one point I said, "You know, both Perimeter and Hopewell are doing some great things serving in the community. What if we were to do it together?"

We showed a video of Sharefest in Little Rock and wondered out loud: "Could this happen in Atlanta?" Little did we know that this conversation between two churches would end up birthing what is now Unite! It started with the vision of our two churches, not the masses.

A few weeks later Perimeter and Hopewell decided to go for it. We did so with a plan to have churches serve together in the community the first weekend in October 2003 in an event much like Sharefest in Little Rock. We made plans to celebrate together at a local arena the next weekend. We were in. We knew we would see this thing through even if our two churches were the only ones on board.

We had about five months to prepare. We began by inviting the churches we already had relationships with to join us. Over the next month or two we developed an initial core group of about eight churches, and we did this through personal invitation to these churches. Victory World Church, a large multicultural church in Norcross, a suburb of Atlanta, joined us as part of the core team. Pastor Bill Sim from New Church Atlanta started to talk with Korean churches about our plans, and Pastor Tony Garcia had a heart to get some Hispanic churches involved. It was amazing to see how early on the Lord brought together churches that were culturally as well as denominationally diverse. It was also encouraging that three large churches in our area—Perimeter, Hopewell, and Victory World— were an integral part of the core team. On a side note, I discovered in the summer of 2004, when I was researching how other cities pulled the body of Christ together, that most city movements were able to get smaller churches involved but rarely the larger churches. It was a blessing that we were able to start with three large churches. Other churches that joined in at the beginning included New Church of Atlanta, the Vineyard Church, and Epic Church.

In addition to getting the core churches on board, we started having informational lunches to share the vision with other churches about this movement and the October events. From the beginning we cast a vision for an ongoing movement in which churches would partner together. This would not be a "one and done" deal. Churches may come together for events, but it is much more challenging to work together in an ongoing way. Once an event is over, churches often go back to a default position, back to a focus on their own church's internal ministry. We knew that if we as a group of churches were going to have a transformational impact, we would have to build long-term relationships and not make an annual event our primary focus.

We were convinced that having an initial event to plan for together would help us gain traction and momentum. It provided something tangible for churches to work on together, and it really helped Unite! get started. It also gave us a reason to spend time together and start building relationships, which is what was most important for the long term. The biggest challenge would come later when the event was over and we needed to build the infrastructure and momentum for a long-term movement.

We Have Liftoff!

In June of 2003, we formed a planning team for the Compassion in Action (CIA) Weekend. We also developed a team for a celebration we planned to have the following weekend. We called this worship time the Heaven on Earth (HOE) celebration. Each of these teams were made up of staff from the eight core churches. For the CIA Weekend we created a packet of information that walked each church through the process of involvement and gave them ideas for how to serve. Our CIA planning team came alongside churches to answer questions and offer help putting together their projects. Churches developed their own projects for the weekend, and some churches joined forces with others in their projects. While churches were able to do whatever they wanted to do in terms of projects, we did have an emphasis that year on public schools, apartment ministry, and at-risk youth.

About thirty churches participated in over seventy-five projects during the first CIA Weekend. That's thirty churches learning first-hand how powerful it can be to partner together. For a number of churches this was instrumental in getting them much more involved in serving in the community. It was also a strong statement to community members that churches care about their needs and are willing to work together to make a difference.

Not much has changed since 2003 in our basic format for the CIA Weekend. Each church plans its own projects, and some churches join together with other churches to do a project. We have no central headquarters for Unite! We do not create projects for churches to do. The Unite! movement *is* the local churches. Each year the CIA Weekend and all the ongoing ministries are driven by local churches and what they do in the community. One of the unique aspects of Unite! is that it is not a separate organization trying to get churches to do its thing; it is local churches who believe we can be more effective working together than we can by operating on our own. It takes nothing away from the local church because it *is* the local church. Unite! takes the beauty of spiritual giftedness and expands it beyond the four walls of one church. "Each one should use whatever gift he has received to serve others, faithfully administering God's grace in its various forms" (1 Peter 4:10 NIV).

The Ultimate Tailgate Event

Before every launch of a space shuttle from pad 39A at Cape Canaveral, the tailgaters stake their claims along the NASA Causeway that spans the Banana River. That's right. Tailgaters. If you've ever watched a shuttle launch at Cape Canaveral, you know what a spectacle it is. That's because for a rocket to take off, its engines must create enough reaction force to counteract the pull of gravity. And for the engines to create that force, there must be a massive amount of fuel burning beneath the rocket.[2] The phrase "the sparks fly" just doesn't do the experience justice. No wonder there's a party on the beach every time it happens.

Dramatic launches evoke dramatic celebrations. Somehow, we knew that. That's why we figured in a Heaven on Earth event in our plans. One week following our launch—the Compassion in Action Weekend—we made big plans to celebrate. It just made sense.

Heaven on Earth

In an article titled "The Real Worship War," Mark Labberton tells about watching a young man leading worship who sang so enthusiastically that he stepped on the toes of the vocalists standing behind him. Not once but several times, the zealous leader trod on the toes of his backup singers and never even noticed that he did it. The story illustrates Labberton's point about worship in today's churches: "The heart of the battle over worship is this: our worship practices are separated from our call to justice and, worse, foster the self-indulgent tendencies of our culture rather than nurturing the self-sacrificing life of the kingdom of God."[3]

One week following the first Compassion in Action Weekend in 2003, five thousand people came together for the Heaven on Earth celebration at the Gwinnett Arena to bridge that separation between worship and justice. Because our celebration was linked to our themes of justice, poverty, family, and education, we left no room for self-indulgence. Because it was in response to what God had wrought the weekend before, our focus was gratitude. Because we partnered together not only to serve but also to sing, we didn't experience the worship wars tension over style that sometimes occurs when musicians plan together. We not only worshiped but also blessed community leaders and took up an offering that went entirely to three organizations in the community who were on the front lines of ministry. We prayed for community leaders. Governor Sonny Perdue spoke and encouraged our churches about uniting and making a difference. It was a powerful evening, and it truly was a picture of heaven on earth as people from many nations and ethnicities celebrated together.

The Heaven on Earth celebration team planned the event. One of the worship pastors took the lead in putting together a combined choir and worship team. We wanted the evening to be not only a visible demonstration of the unity of the body of Christ but also a real blessing to the community and its leaders. The celebration team got input from the senior pastors and put together a great program. It took a lot of effort for a combined choir and worship team to prepare for the evening because everything they did was in addition to what each church was doing for its own worship services, but it was a powerful time for those involved. During the preparation for the event, relationships were forged among the music teams. The weekend of worship was sweet-sounding evidence to both churches and the community that the diverse body can work and worship together.

In a front-page article in the *Atlanta Journal-Constitution* called "A Love That Bridges Barriers," Rick Badie reported on our Heaven on Earth celebration:

> There are some people working to turn the segregated church of the South into a relic.
>
> On Sunday, about 10,000 [the actual number was closer to 5,000] of them gathered at the Arena at Gwinnett Center in Duluth. The blacks, whites, Asians, Latinos and Africans represent Unite—a coalition of churches. . . . They gathered Sunday to celebrate a recent weekend in which they lent a hand to the international community and the needy.[4]

Change Agents

One of the most fascinating sociological studies in the last few decades has been the study of change and how it occurs in society as a whole. Scientists have asked, "What factors contribute to change, and what might cause an entire people group to adopt a new way of acting or thinking?" Several now-familiar phrases have sprung from these studies. In his classic study of the "diffusion of innovation," Everett Rogers looked back on established trends—cell phone ownership, for example—after they had become widespread and examined the people who, over time, adopted that trend.[5] Rogers plotted everyone who ultimately became a part of the majority on a bell curve. On one end there was the slim minority of innovators, closely followed by the early adopters. By far the largest groups were the early majority and the late majority in the middle of the curve. The laggards brought up the rear as the traditionalists who don't accept change readily.

Although we were convinced that community transformation and church partnership were solid biblical values and that God was directing us, we also observed the fundamental human tendency

126

to adopt change slowly. The church has had a "y'all come join the club" approach to the world for a long time; therefore community outreach by a united group of church partners may well be an innovation unique to this generation. Much has been written lately about the need for the church to have a *missional* approach as opposed to the more traditional *attractional* approach. The few churches in northeast Atlanta who deployed their people into the community to do ministry *out there* in 2003 were early adopters of a new trend that is now happening on a larger scale.

If Everett Rogers's observations about people and change are correct, early adopters of something they passionately embrace must learn patience while the rest of the world catches on. And if it is true that the compelling voices of the innovators can sway the majority—eventually—then a movement can begin with just a few people. A church movement can begin with just a few churches. It is important to mention that a movement like Unite! does not have to start with such a big splash. In fact, it can be much simpler to start smaller. The number of churches involved is not the most critical factor in getting started. The key is to cast the vision and then to go with those who are willing, those who freely adopt the idea. That was our commitment. We were prepared to move ahead even if the only churches involved were Perimeter and Hopewell. Over time we began to see the Lord convince pastors and leaders of the kingdom value of partnering. And soon more and more were getting on board.

One final benefit of our Compassion in Action Weekends is that they represent milestones in the growth of the Unite! movement. From 2003 to 2009, the number of churches involved in Unite! grew from 30 to over 150! At Perimeter, we have not widened our twelve-mile radius, but God has clearly widened the work of his kingdom.

Think about it

What is . . .

Is there an event in your city or state that is similar to Sharefest or Compassion in Action where churches work together? Is your church involved?

What could be . . .

Imagine that your church has become a catalyst for healthy, strong relationships among the churches in your community. What initial steps did you take to build those relationships?

Now imagine a significant community initiative planned and produced by the efforts of these churches. Dream for a moment and describe this initiative.

What will be . . .

What are some specific steps you can take over the next six months to build relationships with the people or staff members from other churches?

What are steps you can take to plan and implement an event or initiative together with other churches?

What we did . . .

Preparation for the first Compassion in Action Weekend took about five months. It looked something like this:

- We met with a few pastors and leaders from neighboring churches and showed a video about Sharefest in Little Rock, Arkansas. Perimeter and Hopewell Missionary Baptist decided to do such an event in Atlanta.
- Working through personal invitation and word of mouth, we developed a core team of eight churches during the first two months.
- The core team held informational meetings in restaurants to explain the vision and invite churches to get involved.
- We also developed two teams made up of staff from the eight core churches to plan the Compassion in Action Weekend and the Heaven on Earth celebration the following weekend.
- We developed the church starter packets to give to churches. This enabled a church to plan its own involvement in the Compassion in Action Weekend.

To get more information about Unite! and how churches are working together, go to www.anewkindofbig.com.

Picture This

Homer Hickam was just fourteen years old when he watched the Sputnik satellite orbit over his hometown of Coalwood, West Virginia. The son and grandson of a miner, everyone expected Homer to follow his father's footsteps into the dark duty of coal mining. But that Sputnik flight changed something inside Homer and forever altered the trajectory of his life.

The movie *October Sky* tells the story of Homer's first foray into space: an entry in the local science fair. From the beginning, Hickam's story is one of camaraderie. His first rocket was built with the help of two friends and the high school math geek, along with encouragement from the boys' science teacher at Big Creek High School. The rest, as they say, is history.

Homer Hickam went on to attend Virginia Tech and became a NASA scientist. He also wrote *Rocket Boys: A Memoir*, the *New York Times* best seller on which the movie is based. It's important to note that the "rocket boys" reunite in Coalwood for one weekend every fall for the October Sky Festival, an event that celebrates their accomplishments and the relationships that to this day exist because a bunch of high school boys attempted the impossible.

You might say one launch (Sputnik) instigated another launch (Homer's first rocket) that eventually contributed to many more launches in our country's space program. Launches are like that. They birth something in us. Especially when they happen in the context of friendship.

A rocket won't fly unless somebody lights the fuse.

Homer Hickam

Was it through your know-how that the hawk learned to fly, soaring effortlessly on thermal updrafts? Did you command the eagle's flight, and teach her to build her nest in the heights?

Job 39:26–27 Message

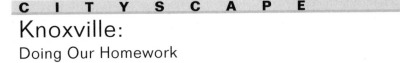

Knoxville:
Doing Our Homework

Giving a Resource to the City

Let's say I want to take my wife on a date next Saturday night. I'm excited about treating her, so I plan ahead. First, I buy tickets to a hockey game. Next, I think about which vendor we'll get dinner from because we won't have time to eat at a restaurant. There's a basketball game on that night too, so I plan for us to stop by a neighborhood sports bar on the way home to watch the second half. I want to give her a gift, so I sneak off to Walmart the day before and buy her a new set of towels (I like them fluffy, and ours are getting old and threadbare). Green is my favorite color, so although I'm pretty sure our bathrooms are blue and pink, I get green.

Just writing this down makes me nervous. That's because I am certain my plan would bomb, and royally so. It is a disastrous scheme because it is backed up by zero data and is driven solely by my own selfish, skewed ideas. I have, in fact, researched my wife over the years. I know what makes her feel special, what types of gifts and restaurants and entertainment would float her boat. I know her. It has taken some time, but I know how to meet her needs. I've done my homework. And I know that an evening of sports, hot dogs, and green towels would meet *my* needs—but not my wife's. Similarly, if the church doesn't do its homework to understand the needs and dreams of the community, we may think we are serving the community when in reality we are serving ourselves.

One city that has been researched thoroughly by the Christian community in order to effectively meet its needs is Knoxville, Tennessee. In 1998, a group of Christians in Knoxville desired to invest in ministries that would make a difference in their city. Andy Rittenhouse was hired by the Knoxville Christian Community Foundation to examine the urgency and scope of the city's social needs. This research was compiled in the first edition of the *Salt and Light Guidebook*, which revealed many needs but also highlighted the sacrificial labors of numerous faith-based community service organizations active in the city. Soon after, a band of Knoxville churches began a dialogue about how to respond to this research by combining their passion and resources to demonstrate God's love to Knoxville's residents. This led to the founding of the Compassion Coalition in 2000 as a network of Christians committed to being salt and light in the Knoxville area (Matt. 5:13–16).

The mission of the Compassion Coalition, which now includes over one hundred churches, is to inform, equip, and connect believers to transform lives and communities through the love of Christ, manifesting the unity of the body of Christ. It does this by conducting and disseminating research on community needs and resources, by training churches for empowering service, and by helping to build collaborative relationships among churches and with community-serving organizations. They are getting to know their community in a way most Christian communities have never attempted. We would do well to learn from them.

The third edition of *Salt and Light: A Guide to Loving Knoxville* was released in 2009.[6] This resource draws on an extensive four-month research process that included twenty-eight focus groups that brought together diverse people working on a variety of concerns; personal interviews; analysis of data from agency reports, the U.S. Census Bureau, internet databases, the local planning commission, and other sources; several special reports commissioned from professional researchers; a survey of area churches; and a survey of residents in public housing communities. Andy Rittenhouse, again, took the lead in conducting and editing this research.

Based on this research, the first half of the book unpacks twenty-nine specific areas of ministry in Knoxville, ranging from foster care to mental health to poverty to racial reconciliation. Essays on each of these issues describe the challenges, lay out a biblically based vision for change, and call the church to an informed, practical response. Each chapter in this section also includes personal stories, background research, ministry examples, prayer points, suggestions for families and churches to get involved, and a list of volunteer opportunities.

Research also plays a prominent role in a section that lays out ten "windows" on Knoxville, describing different perspectives on the city, such as "Religious Knoxville," "Ethnic Knoxville," "Business Knoxville," and "Struggling Knoxville." The book also includes a section on demographics, with detailed tables and maps. Other sections of the book further equip Christians to carry out their role as salt and light in the city: resources on mobilizing the church for ministry, guidelines and case studies for collaborative ministry, and a biblical framework for transformational ministry. Most of the material is by local authors—Knoxville nonprofit leaders, pastors, and freelance writers—with support from a professional research and editorial team. For a more detailed explanation of the process these Knoxville churches and ministries used to do their research, see appendix 4.

Cataloging the Needs and Revealing the Resources

Along the way, the Salt and Light team discovered some things about their city that shocked and dismayed them. For example, they learned that children in over fifteen thousand Knox County households live in a home with only one parent and that almost half of these children in single-parent households live in poverty; that up to eight hundred children experience homelessness in the course of a year; that black infants in Knoxville are three times more likely to die than white infants; and that every week an average of fifteen Knox County children suffer substantiated cases of abuse or neglect.[7]

The sum impact of Knoxville's research could have been despair. The need turned out to be bigger, upon close inspection, than anyone dreamed. But the research doggedly returns time and time again to hope. *Salt and Light* doesn't just catalog the needs; it reveals the resources. It points to the big-enough-to-meet-the-needs expanse of the church: the tens of thousands of followers of Christ in Knoxville who gather in about six hundred congregations. The book reports that the volunteer spirit is alive and well in the Knoxville area, with over 2,000 nonprofit organizations, and 107,200 volunteers who contribute a total of 9.6 million hours of service valued at $194.4 million.[8] It tells many stories of hope of followers of Jesus who are engaging the needs through faith-based ministries and partnerships. It uncovers the assets that are often overlooked within disadvantaged communities. And it points to the big heart of a Creator who never sleeps in his loving pursuit of his creation. It's a reminder not only that we must do research in order to understand our city's current reality but also that we must turn our focus to the "great cloud of witnesses" cheering us on and "fix our eyes on . . . the author and perfecter of our faith" (Heb. 12:1–2 NIV) if we are going to have the right perspective—God's perspective.

While providing a wealth of information about Knoxville, *Salt and Light* underscores that data alone does not provide the church with sufficient knowledge to minister effectively in a community. To get to know my wife, for example, I need more than facts *about* her; I have to spend time *with* her, interacting with her and really listening to her perspective. Similarly, statistical research is important in quantifying needs and resources. But to truly understand the heart of a community, we need to be intentional about building relationships with people, taking the time to get to know their concerns, hopes, and dreams. We also must recognize the diversity of perspectives within a community and learn how to dialogue across boundaries of class, race, language, and life experience.

As *Salt and Light* affirms in the article "Community Study," "A city study with the goal of transformation is not armchair analysis. We approach the community more like getting to know a friend than like studying a subject for a school report."[9] For this reason, the book includes many stories from the lives of people who are struggling, which encourages readers to "walk a mile in another person's shoes" so they can better walk alongside them in ministry. The churches' outreach must value input from the people we serve and reflect their dreams and concerns rather than our own agenda. "Otherwise," says Stanley Taylor with the Knoxville Leadership Foundation, "we are superimposing transformation on them, versus becoming a part of the transformation with them."[10]

Project director Andy Rittenhouse states, "Ultimately, Salt & Light is not about the church or about Knoxville, it's about Jesus. It's about his life and his purpose (see Luke 4:18–19) fleshed out in the lives of his followers spread throughout this community."[11] God's heart for our city compels us to share the love of Christ "with actions and in truth" (1 John 3:18 NIV). We must learn the truth about our city through research in order to help move the church to informed, faithful action.

> Salt is excellent. But if the salt goes flat, it's useless, good for nothing. Are you listening to this? Really listening?
>
> Luke 14:34 Message

> When the kids win, we all win. When they lose, we all lose. We can either build more prisons, or do something else. If we do nothing, we will have to build more prisons and increase acreage in our cemeteries.
>
> Stanley Taylor, Knoxville Leadership Foundation

10

Orbit

Launching Christians into Channels of Influence

After takeoff, then what? For the NASA astronauts who spend two weeks aboard a space shuttle with a fifty-thousand-pound payload, takeoff is just the beginning. It's in orbit that the real work is done. On Mission STS-128, the thirty-seventh mission of Discovery, the space shuttle carried 7.5 tons of supplies inside the Leonardo Multi-Purpose Logistics Module to the International Space Station two hundred miles above earth. The crew also dropped Nicole Stott off at the station, where she replaced Timothy Kopra as Expedition 20 Engineer. Kopra then hitched a ride home on the return flight of Discovery.[1]

Orbits. We know all about them. Orbits are the travelogues of our daily lives. From the route you take to work to the social circles you inhabit to the people you pass by every day, you live your life along the tracks of a few important orbits. Important because they determine how you invest your time, money, and passion. Important because they are, in part, the indicators of what you value. Important because your orbits are the pathways of your influence.

Influence. We know about that too. Whether we intend to or not, we all exert influence. And the most strategic, most authentic, most compelling context for personal influence is our personal orbits. We can't help it. Keep a travel diary of your daily life and you will find your influence, your impact on your world. It may not seem as dramatic or intentional as the mission trip you took last summer or the weekend project you participated in last week, but it's there, and it is more potent than you think. That's because it is—like an orbit—repeated, consistent, continual. Just as the catchy refrain of a song lodges in your brain and becomes impossible to forget, your influence is strongest when it is part of the rhythm of your life.

Right under Our Noses

Like a pilot of a space shuttle who changes his orbit to adjust to an unexpected shift in weather patterns or a meteor shower, we are always looking for new ways to leverage our resources to meet the outer-space-sized needs of our community. We discovered one strategy right in the heart of our own church.

Jesus's mandate to make disciples permeates everything we do at Perimeter Church. Discipleship, perhaps more than any church-growth strategy, is stunning in its simplicity. It isn't particularly complicated. It can be done by anyone anywhere. In fact, it is best done in the context of our orbits. Whenever possible, we have encouraged our people at Perimeter to engage in life-on-life friendships with those in their personal orbits, their workplaces, their neighborhoods. Yes, a more formal discipleship relationship may result, but the power of friendships smack in the middle of everyday life is an overlooked commodity. Rather than dump discipleship into a church setting, why not take it out into your social environment and look for opportunities there? Rather than gather the Christians in your neighborhood or business into isolated huddles for a Bible study, why not free up your time to make friends outside that circle? Why not pray to be an influencer where you live and work? This is stewardship of the orbits God has placed us in.

If life-on-life missional discipleship where we live, work, and play is the most natural conduit for personal transformation, might *community* transformation happen in a similar way? What if we began to examine our orbits as opportunities for even greater influence?

Channels of Cultural Influence

Just as our task force defined the focus of Community Outreach at Perimeter Church in almost every area of our new ministry—partnering, positioning, learning, staffing—we have begun to define the orbits, or channels, of influence that already exist in our community. "Channels of cultural influence" is the term we use for places of employment, commerce, and social service. We have identified eight particular channels: education, health care, business, art and entertainment, media, nonprofits, government, and law/justice. We are still exploring the potential in each of these channels. You might call this networking with a specific focus. Because the influence we hope to leverage in these areas will come through our *relationships*, we cannot predict what will happen when the doors open to these orbits. Our dream is for greater influence both within each channel and across channels as people work together to make a kingdom impact.

The vision we are beginning to cast within our congregation and among Unite! churches goes beyond the personal investment of believers in the lives of people in their personal channels. We urge the restoration of all the nouns—not only persons but also places and things—in that channel. Our desire is to work strategically to influence each channel in such a way that kingdom values and characteristics are reflected in that channel. That's the heart of community transformation. The projects completed during Compassion in Action Weekends and the ministries targeting public schools, hungry children, and needy families all contribute to that goal. But launching people into these cultural channels, or orbits, is a grassroots addition to those efforts. It may well prove to be more than an addition; we've yet to see how powerful this kind of influence can be.

Most traditional "workplace" ministry models in churches place a major emphasis on evangelism in the workplace, usually through means of starting Bible studies, witnessing techniques, etc. Our vision for influencing the channels of cultural influence *includes* evangelism, but it is more holistic in that it is expanded to include this goal: We want every channel to increasingly reflect the characteristics of the kingdom of God. As you can see in the diagram below, each channel is connected to the center, the city. Because families and churches are part of each channel, they are shown here as entities that touch each channel.

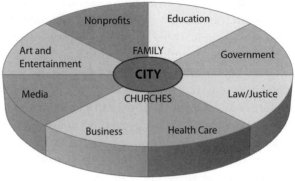

Channels Launch Strategy

At this point, we have made a shift in our philosophy more than a shift in our practice. As we launch the vision for channels of cultural influence, our plan is to place the spotlight on education first. Our local public schools serve as the connecting points of our communities, so it's the most logical place to start. We have already made significant inroads into our area schools through our assistance with tutoring and our service projects in local schools. That means we have stable relationships and open doors.

Our plan is to identify, gather, and equip teachers, administrators, and parents to make an impact in their particular schools. Education is the one channel that crosses over into most every other channel. We plan to invite people, representing every other channel of cultural influence, to discover what role they might play in making a difference in the education channel.

As we launch, we plan to provide vision casting, encouragement, and networking opportunities for anyone interested in finding out how to make a kingdom difference in any of the other channels of cultural influence. Our hope is to help connect people within each channel to each other. As they begin to take ownership of that channel of influence, our intention is to lead them to mobilize others to do the same. In that simple way, leaders will develop.

The following information is an excerpt from the article "City Transformation in China: A Starting Point" by Diana Wang, with Talene Lee, commissioned by ChinaSource. In the article, she describes eight channels for cultural influence that she calls God's domains. She connects each domain to a characteristic, or definition, of God and stresses that the purpose for each of these channels in our cities is his glory. For a fuller treatment of this subject (and Wang's major source material), see Landa Cope, *The Old Testament Template: Rediscovering God's Principles for Discipling All Nations* (Cape Town, South Africa: Template Institute Press, 2007).

Government: Justice—King of Kings

Purpose: to provide an independent and objective source of arbitration and conflict resolution for society and between nations, providing and insuring justice and equality for all citizens.

Family: Nurture and Love—The Heavenly Father

Purpose: to provide a safe, loving, and nurturing environment for growth, values, and education of the next generation.

Church: Mercy and Holiness—The Great High Priest

Purpose: to provide for propagation of the faith and discipleship of all believers in the whole nature and character of God, his Word applied to the work and walk of faith, and to facilitate the expression of that faith in worship, fellowship, and the sacraments of the church.

Science and Technology: Order and Power—The Creator

Purpose: to discover and use God's natural laws in order to bless all of creation by pursuing a higher quality of life, better health, and greater stewardship of God's resources and created universe.

Economics and Business: Provision—God Our Provider

Purpose: to provide the needed goods and services and gainful employment opportunities for the community at large at a fair market price and wage.

Education: Knowledge—The Great Teacher

Purpose: to develop the God-given gifts in every person to their highest potential in the service of their community, believing God gifts every child.

Communication and Media: Truth—The Living Word

Purpose: to provide truthful, objective information of importance to the community at large so that citizens can make informed decisions.

Arts and Entertainment: Beauty—The Potter, the Song of Songs

Purpose: to provide for rest, relaxation, and renewal of the soul through beauty and joy.

Can you envision a society where each of these domains fulfills, even in part, the God-glorifying purpose for which he created it? Isn't it an inspiring picture?

What Went Wrong?

In her book *The Old Testament Template: Rediscovering God's Principles for Discipling All Nations*, Landa Cope examines the history of missions and asks some hard questions: "Nations are being reached, but the quality of life in most is unacceptable. Why? After nearly two centuries of dynamic influence, how has the church in the last two hundred years become so contained? What do we do to restore the power of the gospel to change lives and communities as it has done in history?"[2] Gabe Lyons, coauthor of *unChristian*, has noticed the same themes and has come to similar conclusions: "*Christianity has gained more conversions in America over the last two hundred years than any other faith. Simultaneously, Christianity has steadily lost cultural influence despite its rapid conversion growth.*"[3] Lyons affirms the need for Christians to impact the world through their obedient, personal following of Christ. But he insists there's more:

> The problem is that it is only part of the solution. In a widely distributed briefing that was presented to The Trinity Forum called To Change the World, James Davison Hunter asserts, "It is this view of culture that also leads some faith communities to evangelism as their primary means of changing the world. . . ."
>
> Hunter goes on to say, " . . . the renewal of our hearts and minds is not only important, it is essential, indeed a precondition for a truly just and humane society. But by itself, it will not accomplish the objectives and ideals we hope for." This could explain why Christianity as it is practiced by many well meaning, admirable Christians in the past decades has failed to have significant traction.[4]

Deploying Christians into their channels of influence in the community is one way—one effective and biblical way—to "uncontain" the church and release it into the world. Lyons believes the church in the last century has been guilty of presenting only half of the story to the world. He reminds us that we must tell the full story of the gospel. The full story harkens back to creation and God's original plan. The full story embraces God's heart for restoration, not just redemption. And the full story is holistic, making truth an all-encompassing worldview instead of just another religious system.

Missional Communities

As people connect with one another in common and different channels, they will fold into missional communities, where they can be supported through relationships, resources, and equipping for the purpose of strategic deployment. As we have discovered through the many opportunities to serve through Community Outreach and Unite!, people most naturally develop community around mission. The camaraderie that forms around a kingdom purpose deepens more quickly than the forced relationships of a new small group that meets only for fellowship.

In an interview titled "Small Groups and the Missional Renaissance," Reggie McNeal says, "When we think about 'missional,' almost everyone thinks about running out and painting a school or fixing up some park or something. The problem, of course, is that if that's just an activity layered on top of our other activities, then there really hasn't been a profound shift in focus—just a shift in activity. Being missional moves us from internal concerns to external concerns. We start every question not with 'What are we doing here,' but 'What is our impact out there?'"[5]

Impact involves leadership. We can do more than influence by simply being a part of any given channel. The church has a stockpile of competent leaders inside its walls whom we must begin to scatter in a strategic manner out into the community. If it is true that the gospel brings restoration along with redemption, then we must lead the way in movements of restoration. We can do that by connecting, equipping, and deploying our people in their channels. Transformation will slowly take place if we do. But we must be more than participants in our culture; we must be conveners of change as well.

Conveners of Change

Many of our partner ministries understand this shift in focus. For example, Street GRACE—the nonprofit dedicated to abolishing the sex trade in Atlanta—is much more than a do-good organization. They raise funds, they mobilize churches, they educate, all with a focus on the heinous crime of sex trafficking in our city (Atlanta is considered one of the top cities in the nation for this industry). But Street GRACE does more. This fledgling initiative has already leveraged its considerable influence by becoming a convener of Atlanta's significant leaders in this area. They work across the board, exerting influence in areas of law enforcement, our judicial system, other nonprofits, and churches. From lobbying to street work to "lunch and learn" events with pastors, the staff and volunteers of Street GRACE travel in as many channels as they can. They have learned the wisdom of expanding influence to more than one channel.

In a nationwide move called Operation Cross Country IV, the FBI and local authorities took a big bite out of a big crime.[6] In October of 2009, law enforcement authorities in Atlanta recovered fifty-two children and arrested sixty pimps. More than six hundred people were arrested statewide in this one initiative alone. Street GRACE continually monitors our city's progress in this area. Their website (www.streetgrace.org) tracks actual arrests and legislative changes. There's no way to accurately measure the impact of the church on this issue, but it's hard to miss the connection between the growing influence of the body of Christ in this area and the response of our city's leaders.

Identifying and targeting these cultural channels of influence where people actually live and work provides a track for this shift in focus to run on. When we tie our mission to a greater purpose, we make the goal of our "impact out there" not only a personal renaissance in individuals' lives but also a renaissance of our culture.

Open to the Light

While in space, the crew of Discovery lives in a two-thousand-cubic-foot compartment with three decks. The shuttle is piloted from there, and most activity is controlled from its consoles, but once the vehicle reaches the space station or the altitude necessary for its mission, the workplace is the cargo bay, by far the largest section of the fuselage. That's where the real heavy lifting takes place. Depending upon the need of the mission, an orbiting space shuttle can be oriented to face toward or away from the earth, with the doors open and the payload exposed to either the sun or the earth. Those doors are fit-ted with thermal radiators that act as part of the vehicle's climate control system.

Radiating the sun's light and warmth—that's what can happen in orbit when we are positioned to do so. The church has had this as its mission from the beginning: to turn our faces to the Son and absorb his light, then turn toward the world to reflect that same light. While community transformation can happen in a number of ways, the intentional use of our orbits—such as education, health care, business, arts and entertainment, media, nonprofits, government, and law/justice—positions us to reflect the Light in strategic ways. Unite! has just explored the tip of the iceberg here. We have energetically served our community in as many ways as we can find, and we're discovering that the capacity of the body of Christ is boundless and the creativity of our sovereign Lord is breathtaking. Who knows what doors will open as we look for new ways to impact our community and our culture?

Think about It

What is . . .

What is your church doing to encourage and equip your people to make kingdom impact in their channels of cultural influence?

How is your church helping people of similar passions and interests find one another within the church for the purpose of influencing their channels outside the church?

What could be . . .

Imagine the transformation not just of people in your community but of the culture of that community.

What were the critical factors that led to your church effectively deploying its people into the channels?

What were some challenges you had to overcome?

What will be . . .

What strategic steps will you and your church need to take to effectively equip, connect, and deploy your people for kingdom impact in the channels? (To get you started, think of the list of channels of cultural influence Perimeter Church has identified: education, health care, business, arts and entertainment, media, nonprofits, government, and law/justice.)

What is the most important thing you need to do in the next six months to move your church in this direction?

What we did . . .

You may have noticed that I have referenced more books and articles in this chapter than in previous ones. That's because we are still in the beginning stages of this approach. We are changing our thinking before we change our doing. We have identified the channels in our city, and we have begun to do what we did before we started Community Outreach or Unite!: think and plan and build relationships. We are also stepping up our connections with partners who understand the need to impact people *and* culture, like Street GRACE.

Picture This

The human creations that most clearly mimic the stars and their grandeur are hand-cut diamonds. Unlike stars, uncommon miracles we commonly see almost every night, diamonds are rare, but like stars, they were first created by God alone in the mysterious dark. And then humans get involved. It takes more than one industry to produce a diamond necklace. To create an exquisite adornment out of precious metals and nearly priceless jewels, a concert of effort is needed. First, the raw diamond is mined from its deep hiding place in the earth, then the artisans go to work. From the lapidary who cuts and polishes and engraves the stones to the designer who conceives the arrangement of those stones to the jeweler trained in soldering, metal fabrication, and casting, who puts it all together, the final work of art is a creative collaboration. Stand back to admire a diamond necklace, as the many facets reflect light like so many stars, and you can't help but make the comparison between the human creation and the heavenly one. The impact is stunning.

When we work in concert with others to create impact, we're all part of the artistry (because that's what kingdom impact is after

144

all, a well-crafted influence). And the effect of our work—no matter where we sit on the assembly line—has the potential to shine.

> Those who are wise will shine like the brightness of the heavens, and those who lead many to righteousness, like the stars for ever and ever.
>
> Daniel 12:3 NIV

> The hues of the opal, the light of the diamond, are not to be seen if the eye is too near.
>
> Ralph Waldo Emerson

Atlanta:
Big Starts Small

Opening the Schoolroom Door

Long before Unite! was a gleam in anyone's eye, I had this thought: Maybe the way to change a community was to begin in the one place the community cared about most, the one place the people in our neighborhoods were most passionate about, most invested in. It would be years before my own family had any personal interest in this huge hub of society, but somehow I knew it was a key to community transformation. I would not have called it a "cultural channel of influence" back then, but I knew that's exactly what it was.

Public schools. Want to measure the level of poverty in your county? Simply track the number of free and reduced lunches in your public schools. That's where the changing demographics of any area show up on the radar first. Our public schools are the alarm system for our communities, if we'll just listen.

It wasn't until I became the Community Outreach director at Perimeter Church that I realized the connection between schools and the entire community. As a middle school pastor, I had made it a practice to hang out with kids on their turf, and that meant their schools. I knew if I wanted to reach kids, I had to go where they were. When my role changed at the church and I was no longer focused on teenagers, I still found myself drawn back into the schools. I began mentoring students at a local elementary school. I was struck by

146

the difference just thirty minutes a week could make in one child's life. This was long before education was identified as one of our four impact areas. For me, reaching out to kids at school was more instinctive—a function of years of middle school ministry—than strategic, but it wasn't long before it became strategic in a big way. Strategic . . . and personal.

We—my family and I—live within that critical twelve-mile radius around Perimeter Church. That means the shifting cultural changes addressed by Unite! are outside the back door of our home as well as our church, and these issues begin and end at our public schools. Perimeter School, our church's top-notch K–8th grade school, seemed to be the best place for our two children. As caring parents, it just made sense to send them there. Our oldest started at Perimeter and flourished.

But we were compelled by a mission, a mission so large it couldn't be contained by a job or an eight-hour day, a mission so big it demanded entrance into all of life. It wasn't my mission; otherwise my family would have remained on the sidelines cheering me on. It was their mission too. Community transformation eventually became so much a part of our lives in the present and our dreams for the future that we had to consider it in every decision, including where our kids went to school.

Today both our daughter and our son are in public school. Our daughter made the transition after fifth grade, and our son has never known anything else. My wife and I are both involved in leadership at the kids' schools. I help lead an All Pro Dad chapter at our son's school that encourages dads and other males to get involved in their sons' schools. We helped start WyldLife (the middle school version of Young Life ministry) at our daughter's school. My wife participates in Moms In Touch prayer groups at both schools. Our primary friendships are with the families we've encountered through these schools. Because of this pivotal choice to place our kids in public schools, we have become part of our community in ways we never would have otherwise, and we have developed a heart for this part of the city. It isn't just a demographic or an idea to us anymore; it is real people and a real place.

All Because of Public Schools

My wife and I are convinced we are able to be salt and light to our community in powerful ways simply because we are involved in the public schools. That doesn't mean every Christian family has to do it this way. It doesn't mean the other education options are wrong or subpar. It's just our story. But our story does parallel the story of Unite! We've seen our family's tiny microcosmic influence multiplied many times over as churches in our city have united to serve the public schools.

The leadership at Unite! began asking local principals, "What one thing could the church do for you?" The answer every time: mentor our children. Most schools have a tutoring/mentoring program already set up, but they are usually dealing with a small volunteer base consisting of mostly parents in that school. And most schools need so much more than that. What a simple way to serve schools. I already knew personally the value of investing thirty minutes once a week in one child's life. What if we rallied the community—churches, organizations, businesses—to volunteer for a program already in place in their public schools?

Not long ago we established Half Hour Heroes as a promotional arm for the schools and a call to action to the church. Not just churches are involved; businesses are beginning to respond by sending five, ten, or fifteen people into the schools to tutor kids. We're finding it is easy to be a hero to a child in school. This program is fairly new, but it echoes everything we've done until now, and it provides laserlike focus for our broader focus on education.

Even before we nailed down our four impact areas for Unite!, we began an adopt-a-school program. Today seventy-five schools have been adopted by churches. Our dream is for a church to adopt every school in our city. We suspected education had the potential to be the widest channel of influence in our culture. An article in 2005 in the *Atlanta Journal-Constitution* convinced us we were on the right track:

> Prayer may not have a place in the public schools, but prayerful people do.

That was the message to pastors in a coalition of Gwinnett, Fulton, Cobb and DeKalb churches who met Friday to launch an Adopt-A-School program. The idea is for churches to send their members into the schools—not as religious missionaries but as volunteer tutors, teachers' assistants and anything else the schools need to boost their struggling students.

The Adopt-A-School concept got high marks from Louise Radloff, a member of the Gwinnett Board of Education. "I'll take any help that will make a difference in the lives of our children," she said. Though Radloff said she is a firm believer in the separation of church and state, she believes this program does not cross any constitutional lines.

"The churches don't have an agenda. They don't have to preach," she said. However, she added, when the volunteers give of their time to help a student, those actions model religious values such as integrity, honesty and caring for others. "That kid is going to come on board and follow," she said. . . .

Overall, the students in the special tutoring programs have experienced a jump of 2.5 years in their reading levels over the past year. . . . Anji Bowers, a teacher at Meadow Creek Elementary, said the efforts of volunteers from the church and elsewhere were instrumental in getting her school removed from the federal "Needs To Improve" list.[7]

When our family turned the key and opened the door to the public schools in our own neighborhood, we left the fortress of a safe, sheltered life inside the walls of church and discovered a vast kingdom potential outside that fortress. That's the heart of Unite!—to find the open doors in the community, doors that lead to "life on the outside," where the world awaits the transforming touch of the body of Christ. The door we chose to open first? The schoolroom door.

The philosophy of the school room in one generation will be the philosophy of government in the next.

Abraham Lincoln

And whoever welcomes a little child like this in my name welcomes me.

Matthew 18:5 NIV

11

Measuring Success

Preparing the Thanksgiving Feast

Let's spend a minute talking about grace, because in a few paragraphs I'm going to bring up some typically ungracelike words, words like *results* and *measurements*. We need to begin with grace.

As I mentioned before, I tend to be competitive. I relish accolades, and I like finish lines, markers of success. I love that rush of adrenaline in the homestretch. In many cases, this God-given drive serves me well and operates as a gift from him. But it's amazing how easy it is to use measures of ministry "success"—numbers in attendance at our events, responses to our words, momentum of our programs—to quantify my worth. In every arena of life where scores are kept, numbers are accounted for, and progress is monitored (that would cover just about everywhere), grace is often edged out by a works-based value system. Ministry is no different. It's easy to think performance is everything.

But the Word teaches us otherwise. Grace means this: Even if I maxed out in ministry, performed with perfection, helped lead Perimeter Church and Unite! to the outer realms of success by any standard, I would not be loved more by God, not one iota more. Nor would my standing with him change. Ephesians 2:8–9 spells it out: "For it is by grace you have been saved, through faith—and this not from yourselves, it is the gift of God—not by works, so that no one can boast" (NIV). We're all familiar with the next verse and its not-so-subtle reminder to take this grace and get moving in good deeds, but our *acceptance* by God into his kingdom is by faith alone, and even that faith is a gift from him. The good works mentioned in Paul's next breath find their genesis, their seed, in a forgiven, grace-granted heart. So grace is where it all begins.

Verse 10 of Ephesians 2 could well describe the reason for Unite! "No, we neither make nor save ourselves. God does both the making and saving. He creates each of us by Christ Jesus to join him in the work he does, the good work he has gotten ready for us to do, work we had better be doing" (Message). Good work is what we were made to do. Here's the irony: As I have immersed myself in the good work Christ invited me to join him in doing, I have become more aware of my need for his grace. As I have sought to lead the church to do what it was created to do, I have become even more aware of our collective need of grace. That's because, while the measurements show improvement and progress, the job is still big and we are still small. Grace is what keeps me from being overwhelmed.

As C. H. Spurgeon said over one hundred years ago, "I believe, that the work of regeneration, conversion, sanctification and faith is not an act of man's free will and power, but of the mighty, efficacious and irresistible grace of God." I concur. I agree wholeheartedly with John Newton, who declared, "When I was young, I was sure of many things now there are only two things of which I am sure. One is, that I am a miserable sinner and the other, that Christ is an all-sufficient Saviour. He is well-taught who learns these two lessons."

Why Measure? A Biblical Answer

Grace is a given, but what does that really mean in my life? Do I "sin so that grace may abound"? Not on your life, or according to Paul, "By no means!" (Rom. 6:15 NIV). Anyone who has embraced God's grace in Christ knows that grace doesn't paralyze us; it propels us. The astounding fact of grace is that we now share in "the divine nature" (2 Peter 1:4 NIV). If that doesn't rev our engines to do the same kinds of works God does, I don't know what will. Peter describes the outworking of this new nature of ours in an almost mathematical way. A momentum is described here, as if godliness is an overflowing equation:

> For this very reason, make every effort to add to your faith goodness; and to goodness, knowledge; and to knowledge, self-control; and to self-control, perseverance; and to perseverance, godliness; and to godliness, brotherly kindness; and to brotherly kindness, love. For if you possess these qualities in increasing measure, they will keep you from being ineffective and unproductive in your knowledge of our Lord Jesus Christ.
>
> 2 Peter 1:5–8 NIV

The biblical pattern is to check up on ourselves from time to time. The goal is to be effective and productive in our knowledge of Christ. *That* we can know him at all is a gift of grace. Getting to know him and becoming like him is a process, an assessable process. Verse 9 makes clear what happens in the life of a believer who doesn't grow, who doesn't produce a modicum of results: "If anyone does not have them [these qualities], he is nearsighted and blind, and has forgotten that he has been cleansed from his past sins" (NIV). In other words, while I am indeed forgiven, my lack of growth renders me forgetful of that forgiveness. Staying at a standstill in my personal spiritual growth can give me grace-amnesia. On the other hand, the more I grow, the more I remember grace.

Keeping track of our own growth is—ironically—a means of stabilizing ourselves on the firm ground of grace. Peter goes on to say in verse 10, "Therefore, my brothers, be all the more eager to make your calling and election sure" (NIV). The word *sure* is rooted in the word for "basis," meaning stable, fast, or firm. Our "calling and election" are rooted in grace, but the way to make our *grasp* of that truth secure is to grow in ways we can measure.

Why Measure? A Practical Answer

Jim Herrington of Mission Houston tells a story that is, in one particular, similar to ours in Atlanta. He says that in the first six years of their collaborative ministry they focused almost solely on building relationships. Just like us, they were convinced this was vital. If the decay of their city—a forty-year decline that seeped into every major arena of Houston's culture—was going to be effectively addressed, the church would have to come together. It was only in the context of authentic, trusting relationships that the gaps between evangelicals and charismatics, Protestants and Catholics, the many cultures and language groups, and men and women could be bridged. It couldn't be done without unity.

Along the way were those who advised them to figure out ways to track and measure their success. Jim says, "For a variety of reasons we didn't do that. Over time that came to haunt us. It resulted in what some in the business world call 'crisis in investor confidence.'" By then Mission Houston was accompanied by "a great cloud of witnesses." Not only were local churches involved, but much of their funding came through the donations of individuals from those churches who work in the private sector. For these people—the vast majority of Mission Houston's benefactors—anecdotal reporting just wasn't enough. "Their call for clarity about tracking and measuring things began as a suggestion and grew steadily to heartfelt cry."[1]

In 2008, the community outreach leaders in Houston repented of their resistance to this advice. They spent a year clarifying and refining their measures for success. Their goals are similar to ours: the spiritual and social transformation of their city. That means tracking progress will have to be long term. Factors such as the divorce rate, the number of people coming to faith, and the decline in the poverty rate are included in their new process. As an example of how this looks, following are the measures they will track in the coming years for their Whole and Healthy Children Initiative:

1. The number of communities that launch an initiative. Our goal is to launch in at least five to six communities in school year 2007/2008 and to increase that every year until we have an initiative in all forty-five communities across the greater Houston area.
2. In each community where an initiative is in place, our goal is to have:

- one hundred mentors for one hundred children in three schools with high percentages of at-risk kids
- one hundred intercessors praying for each of the mentors and the children they are mentoring
- an annual campus beautification project in each school
- $10,000 raised from the private sector for the faculty and administration of each school

Unite! shares this commitment to make periodic calculations of success. Like the leaders of Mission Houston, we are paying closer attention to our progress now than we did when we first got started. For us, it is not enough to attempt community transformation. We want to know if we have achieved it. We want to know how far we've come and how far we have to go. Our means of analyzing outcomes is imbedded in our 2020 vision.

We created the following table in 2009. Its primary purpose is to help us look forward, but in order to do so, we looked back. The 2005–2007 actual numbers were gathered from the U.S. Census Bureau, the FBI, the GBI (Georgia Bureau of Investigation), the Department of Education, and other sources. This is information anyone can find with relative ease on the internet. Please note that this does not represent exhaustive research but rather an attempt to define the condition of our community in broad strokes.

Atlanta 2020 Vision
Measures—Metro Atlanta

Statistic	2005–2007 Actual	2010 Actual	2015 Actual	2020 Goal
Family	National—43 percent divorce rate (national figures—2001)			Reduce divorce rate by 30 percent
Justice	Approximately 400 girls per month prostituted (figures probably much higher)			All children are safe; no children in child sex slavery

Statistic	2005–2007 Actual	2010 Actual	2015 Actual	2020 Goal
Education	70 percent graduation rate (2005) in public schools			95 percent graduation rate from high schools
	69 percent (2006) of third-grade children at grade level			95 percent of third-grade children at grade level
Poverty	40 percent of students free and reduced lunch			20 percent of students free and reduced lunch

How will we fill in the "actual" blanks in this chart? We have decided to let our community do that for us. The next census (2010) will give us more accurate data than any we could gather on our own. This will also give us a perspective that is impossible to skew. The data will not be filtered through our "church eyes" or wishful thinking about results. We hope to compare the figures from 2005–2007 with the upcoming census data. Because we did not define these outcome goals until as late as 2009, we plan to consider the 2010 numbers our baseline for any future measurement.

Even so, measuring outcomes is as much an art as a science. Only time will tell us whether our tracking methods are accurate. We agree with Jim Herrington: "Are these the right measures? Time will tell. But they are the measures to which we believe the Lord has led us and for which we are going to be accountable."[2] We make no excuse for the rather bold aspirations we've embraced here. Just because we are going to measure our efforts doesn't mean we'll grade on a curve in order to look good to others or feel good about our "score." We're constantly reminded of our pastor's admonition to attempt such big things for God that they are doomed to fail if he is not in them. We can shoot high because everything we are and everything we do are stabilized by grace.

Outcome Measurement

Let's say you have a field and you've just planted a soybean crop. You've never planted soybeans; you've always planted corn. At harvesttime, you ask the question, "How many pounds of soybeans did I harvest?" Yes, your attention is drawn to the many factors that either contributed to or detracted from the end result—rainfall, soil condition, pest control—but the bottom line of all your labor is the quantity produced. You have to know what's in your storehouses. If the crop is thin, you may go back to corn next year, but if it is what you hoped for and more, you'll keep at it. This is *outcome* measurement. Our 2020 vision measures the success of Unite! in the same way. It tracks the bottom line, the end result of our work.

Deployment Measurement

Another way to measure your success as a farmer is to keep track of your labor and your laborers. How many showed up? How long did they work? How hard did they work? Regardless of the crop, you definitely need to know the status of your workforce.

On the local church level, specifically at Perimeter Church, we've learned that an important way to measure success is to look not at outcomes but at deployment. How is our workforce doing? Yes, we are interested in the harvest, but we want to know how the harvesters are doing too. Deployment is what happens when believers, motivated by the love of Christ and empowered by the Holy Spirit, use their gifts, talents, and training to love and serve people where they live, work, and play.

The risk of measurement is that it not only highlights successes but also points to failures. I don't want to sound like a glass-half-empty kind of guy, but when Jesus pointed to the fields and noted that they were white and ready for harvest, he was pointing to something *undone*, something God's people had not yet accomplished. And yet his commentary about the harvest is much less an observation of failure than it is a challenge to pray and to get moving. Isn't that what we do when we haven't yet achieved a goal? We pray and get moving. We regroup. Our hope, as we take stock of both our outcomes and the workers deployed to produce those outcomes, is to look at the ways we fall short as opportunities to regroup. To adjust and adapt. To pray and get moving.

Atlanta 2020 Story

Yet another way to chart the future is to write a story. The following is part of a "future vision" story Unite! leadership wrote in an effort to look ahead to the next decade. Our hope is to read this again in 2020 and affirm our hopes for the transformation of our city.

Unite!—Churches Partnering for Transformation

One of the primary reasons for the mobilization of believers all over the city with a kingdom mind-set is churches intentionally working together through Unite! It started with a few churches in 2003 and is now a network of churches spread all over metro Atlanta.

Multiplying around the City

Local churches in leadership in five different regions of Atlanta have taken ownership of impacting their area of the city. Because all the regions are connected together, churches have a common vision and have been intentional about training up leaders from their churches in the various domains for kingdom impact.

The focus is now more on equipping their flock for community and city servant leadership than just training for leadership within the four walls of the church. Churches working together and with other community groups and leaders have also been very effective in addressing strategic areas of opportunity in the city such as at-risk youth.

Neighborhoods Impacted

The partnering is even happening at the neighborhood level where neighbors who go to different churches are working together to love their neighbors in word and deed, and the church is growing as people are loved into the kingdom through their neighbors.

A Time to Celebrate

Harvest is a wonderful word. It conjures up images of a cornucopia spilling over with fruits and vegetables, of multiple hues and flavors, of the dance of purpled feet in the winepress. It is a picture of bounty. Like the word *fruit*, we don't give the biblical word *harvest* the credit it is due. Yes, it refers to salvation. Yes, it is the result of evangelism, but think about who God is and what he's up to in our world. In the context of transformation, harvest is the result of God's touch of restoration on his creation. When fields are "white unto harvest," that means they are bursting with potential, a mass of golden wheat or yellow corn blazing and rippling in the autumn sunlight, ready for the harvester to get to work and bring in the crop.

Movement of Prayer

Through Unite!, deep relationships among staff and the laity have developed, and we now experience a greater atmosphere of partnering among churches rather than competition.

Pastors and others from different churches are praying together and supporting one another in incredible ways. Pastor prayer clusters gather all over the city. Moms In Touch prayer groups have tripled over the last ten years. Pastors are meeting together regularly with community and city leaders to pray for and with them. The combination of relationship and dependency on God has been powerful. A sense of urgency and expectation permeates our churches.

Churches Respond during Atlanta Disasters

Possibly the most powerful Christian witness to the community and the main reason for church growth has been the response of believers to major disasters that impacted Atlanta over the last ten years. In each case, as hundreds of thousands of families were affected, churches responded quickly in working together with other groups in the city to come alongside these families and walk with them through these tragedies and practically love them.

When many people panicked and isolated and quarantined themselves, believers were often the ones who stayed with and ministered to the sick. The light of Christ shone so brightly that nonbelievers were drawn by significant numbers to Christ.

Atlanta is a very different place than it was fifteen years ago! It sure seems much more like "thy kingdom come on earth as it is in heaven."

In every culture, harvest is a time to work hard followed by a season of feasting, celebrating, and—if the harvest is plentiful—gratitude. It is an excuse for revelry, a party just waiting to happen. This is perhaps the best reason to measure our work. Tracking results isn't exam time; it's festival time. It's Thanksgiving at its finest. At Unite! we're determined not to miss out on the celebration.

Think about It

What is . . .

How does your church currently track the success of its ministries?

Do you measure your ministry in the community? If so, how? What does the community measure?

What could be . . .

Take a moment to describe the impact of the church (yours and others) in your community. Instead of using prose, create an outcomes measurement to show the changes in your community.

What will be . . .

How can you avoid the mistakes of other ministries who neglected to track their progress adequately (Mission Houston and, to some degree, Unite! in Atlanta)? What outcomes can you begin to measure *now*?

How might you use the 2010 census reports to find out what kind of impact you have made or need to make in your city?

What we did . . .

What we have done *so far* is take measurements to use for comparison in the future. We performed our initial research primarily for the purpose of informing our decisions.[3] When the 2010 census data is made public, we will compare the current conditions in Atlanta to the way things were when we started.

The more we can use community-generated data, the better. For example, Street GRACE and others have used the research about sex trafficking conducted by former Atlanta mayor Shirley.[4] The resulting data has provided a ground zero against which Street GRACE and other partner ministries measure change in our city.

Picture This

To fill one bottle of wine takes anywhere from 440 to 660 grapes—crushed, that is, and fermented. That's a lot of trouble for just one bottle. One can't help but wonder who dreamed up the idea in the first place.

Good ideas usually have histories. If they are really good ideas, they pass the test of time. The collaborators who developed ancient projects like the delicate art of winemaking joined hands across time, centuries even. That's how ideas evolve into better ideas. Synergy doesn't just happen in the present tense; it is handed down as well as handed across.

Winemaking is one of those ideas, or innovations, that has evolved for millennia. Historians claim it predates recorded history. In the Bible, it first shows up in Genesis around 2100 BC when Noah plants an antediluvian vineyard, makes wine from its grapes, drinks it, and finds himself in a compromising situation. It's hard not to speculate that this may have been the very first instance of grape fermentation, and therefore unsuspecting Noah didn't know what effect that sour juice would have on him.

Regardless of who discovered the process, winemaking has developed over time into a worldwide agricultural specialty, a multimillion-dollar industry, a science, and a serious hobby. Whether you'll never touch the stuff or you've built a wine cellar in your basement, you have to admit that the production and consumption of wine has been part of our culture for a long, long time. When grape harvesttime comes in Provence or Napa Valley or Chile, it is a celebration with a rich history that reaches back thousands of years. You'd think the process of winemaking would be a static one, but it isn't. The basic idea is prehistoric, but the methods are always improving.

It seems the church is always learning the ancient art of the harvest. We're still honing our methods. Thankfully, we can learn from each other, but we have more than our relationships in the now; we have a two-thousand-year history of harvesting to teach us how it's done.

> When he saw the crowds, he had compassion on them, because they were harassed and helpless, like sheep without a shepherd. Then he said to his disciples, "The harvest is plentiful but the workers are few. Ask the Lord of the harvest, therefore, to send out workers into his harvest field."
>
> Matthew 9:36–38 NIV

> You called, You cried, You shattered my deafness, You sparkled, You blazed, You drove away my blindness, You shed Your fragrance, and I drew in my breath, and I pant for You.
>
> Augustine

A man is not saved against his will, but he is made willing by the operation of the Holy Ghost. A mighty grace which he does not wish to resist enters into the man, disarms him, makes a new creature of him, and he is saved.

C. H. Spurgeon

12

Making Music

The Song Swells as We Partner with Others

On Easter Sunday 1742, a milestone in the history of music and in the life's work of one man was performed at the Musick Hall in Dublin. Citing this night and this musical offering, Ludwig van Beethoven called that man "the greatest composer that ever lived." Like a long-anticipated movie release today, the buzz surrounding the debut of this one piece of music was intense. Women were asked to wear dresses "without hoops" in order to make "room for more company." The music hall's attendance, as expected, set a record that night. The audience was hypnotized as a singer intoned the solemn opening line:

Comfort ye, comfort ye my people, saith your God.

Today the *Messiah* is George Frideric Handel's most recognizable composition. Written as an Easter piece, it is now a fixture of the Christmas season. But whenever and wherever it is performed, its impact is big. The theme—spanning the birth of Christ to the resurrection—is big. The music itself is big. The human response to the music is big. One conductor says, "The feelings of joy you get from the Hallelujah choruses are second to none." Agreed. *Messiah* measures large by just about any standard.

Handel wrote the *Messiah* for a very practical reason. Until 1742, the bulk of Handel's compositions were operas. Operas were his bread and butter. They were what made him famous, but they were elaborate and therefore expensive to produce. They showcased one or two performers who tended to be difficult to manage—we would call them divas today. The set designs had become more intricate and sophisticated and therefore a lot of trouble. Handel had more music in his heart to give to the world, and he simply grew tired of sharing his gifts in a way in which the other elements often obscured the music. To Handel, the music was the thing. The music alone was the offering.

But for music to make its mark on the world, it must make its way from the score to the stage by *some* means. To parlay the music of the *Messiah* to the listeners of his day in as pure a form as possible, Handel chose the simple oratorio. By using the oratorio as his medium, Handel at once reduced the production—jettisoning everything but the choir and the orchestra—*and* expanded it. He partnered with many voices and many instruments to create a musical production that allowed the music—the main thing—to swell to epic proportions.

Have you ever been to a *Messiah* sing-along? Atlanta offers several every year during the Christmas season, usually hosted by local churches or our own symphony orchestra. They are exhilarating and intimidating at the same time. The professionals—the conductor, the chorus, and the orchestra—typically don't make any concessions for the amateurs other than the huge one they've already made by allowing us mere mortals to sing along in the first place. If you can keep up, great. If not, just enjoy the music and wait for an easier spot in the stream of sound to jump back in. It is quite an experience. Blending voices to make music. In the end, it doesn't matter if your voice is weak or strong. No one knows if you are on or off key. The blending erases your mistakes and carries them away. And the blending creates an outcome that humbles you with its beauty and power. You, who may hardly dare to sing in the shower lest someone hear you, are a part of something so big it takes your breath away. In the end, there is no audience, only voices. There are no professionals, only people. The size of your voice doesn't matter. The impact is the music. And what music it is! Exhilarating and intimidating. But mostly exhilarating. That has been our experience of Unite! How could it be otherwise? We began by wondering . . .

> How can Perimeter Church extend the hand of Christ into our neighborhood?
>
> How can we attempt to transform our community?
>
> How can we turn our hearts inside out for the least and the lost?

In the process, we discovered that the music was so big and so beautiful it couldn't be sung alone. Imagine the *Messiah* as a trio? No, we were tasked with something too big for us, something that required more than one church could do alone. To transform a city with the music of God's very Person and his purpose, we had to join with others who knew the tune.

The Choir and the Orchestra

An oratorio gets its musical punch from two groups: the choir and the orchestra. At the risk of leaving someone out, I want to introduce you to both the choir and the orchestra of Unite! I want you to see what God has wrought through a few relationships among churches, relationships that grew to become a movement. Following is a list of the churches and ministries of Unite! Glance over the list with the knowledge that, by the time you read it, it will have changed.

Churches of Unite!

Central City

Atlanta

Cascade UMC
Chapel of Christian Love
City Church Eastside
Daystar International Christian Fellowship

Elizabeth Baptist Church
First Baptist Atlanta
Indonesian Baptist Mission Church
Midtown Community Church
New Church of Atlanta—Korean/pan Asian
New Life Baptist Church—Korean

North Avenue Presbyterian Church
Northside Community Evangelical Free Church
Peachtree Presbyterian Church
Pleasant Word Fellowship Church
Providence Missionary Baptist
St. James UMC
St. Paul's Presbyterian Church
Trinity Vineyard
World Changers Church International
World Fellowship Church International

Decatur

All Souls Fellowship
Total Grace Christian Center
Veritas Church

Dunwoody

All Saints Catholic Church
Dunwoody Baptist Church
Dunwoody Community Church
Dunwoody United Methodist
Kingswood United Methodist

Gainesville

Westminster Presbyterian Church

Roswell

Fellowship Bible Church
First Christian Church
La Iglesia Comunidad Cristiana
Raise His Praise Worship Center
Roswell United Methodist

North Central

Alpharetta

Alpha Community Church
Atlanta Chinese Christian Church North
Christ the Redeemer Church
Grace North Atlanta
Highlands Church
LifePoint Christian Church
The Lord's House Community Church
Mount Pisgah United Methodist Church
Northside Family Worship Center
Open Door Community Church
Restoration Church of God
St. James United Methodist Church

Cumming

First Baptist Cumming
Grace Fellowship
Metropolitan Church of God
Mountain Lake Church
The Vine Community Church

Doraville

Iglesia Bautista El Calvario
Iglesia Bautista Hispana Emanuel
Iglesia Cristiana Emanuel

Northeast

Buford

Destiny Church
Kingdom Life International
Living Faith Church

Dacula

GracePointe Church
Hope Associate Reformed Presbyterian Church
New Branch Community Church

Duluth and Johns Creek

El Calvario Hispanic
Church of the Hills
Cross Pointe Church
Duluth First Baptist
Duluth First United Methodist
Epic Faith
Friendship Baptist
Indonesian Baptist Mission Church
Johns Creek Christian Church
Johns Creek United Methodist
Korean Church of Atlanta UMC
New Beginnings Fellowship
Old Peachtree Presbyterian
Perimeter Church
Sugarloaf UMC

Vietnamese Sunrise Baptist Church
West Gwinnett Christian Church
Westminster Presbyterian Church
World Fellowship Church International

Lawrenceville

12Stone Church
Christ Fellowship Church Atlanta
Christian City Church
The Church at Webb Gin
First United Methodist
Grace Community Church
Grace International Church
International House of Prayer
Lawrenceville Church of God
McKendree UMC
New Gate International Church
North River Community Church
Sword of Truth Apostolic Ministries
Trinity Life Church

Lilburn

Berkmar United Methodist Church
Camp Creek Primitive Baptist Church
Central Baptist Church
City Harvest Worship Center
Community Church of Christ
Harmony Grove United Methodist Church
Harvest Community Church
Lilburn Alliance Church
Living Waters Christian Fellowship
New Life AME Church
New Mercies Christian Church

Norcross

Atlanta Chinese Christian Church North
Atlanta Vineyard Church
Christ Fellowship Church
Christ the King Lutheran
Full Circle Christian Ministries
Glover Baptist Church
Holy Ghost Pastored Bible Church
Hopewell Missionary Baptist
New Generation Missionary Church
Norcross First Baptist Church
Norcross First United Methodist Church

Northeast Community Church
Open Door Community Church—Asian/
American
Peachtree Corners Baptist Church
Peachtree Corners Christian Church
Peachtree Corners Presbyterian
Restoration of Hope World Ministries
Siloam Korean Church of Atlanta
Simpsonwood United Methodist Church
Solid Rock Church Atlanta
Victory World Church

Snellville

Annistown Road Baptist Church
Grace Fellowship Church
Iglesia Bautista Hispana Emanuel
La Nouvelle Jerusalem Atlanta
Snellville First United Methodist Church
Westminster Presbyterian Church

Stone Mountain

Messiah's World Outreach Ministries
La Nouvelle Jerusalem Atlanta

Sugar Hill

Cross Connection Church
The Family Church—FBC Sugar Hill
Grace Church of Gwinnett

Suwanee

Antioch Assemblies of God Church
The Bridge Church
Shadowbrook Baptist Church
Suwanee Parish UMC

Tucker

Atlanta Chinese Christian Church
Little Miller Baptist Church

Northwest

Austell

Austell First UMC
Austell Presbyterian
Ewing Road Baptist
Milford Church of God

New Genesis Church
Olive Springs Baptist Church
Orange Hill Baptist Church
Victorious Church

Mableton

First Christian Church of Mableton
Vinings Lake Church
Westside Baptist Church

Marietta

Bethany Korean Presbyterian Church
CrossBridge Church
Destiny Metropolitan Worship Center
East Cobb Presbyterian
Grace Community Presbyterian
Johnson Ferry Baptist Church
Life's Hope Church
Mt. Paran N. Church of God
Refuge West Church

Powder Springs

Trinity Chapel

Smyrna

Cumberland Community Church
Hurt Road Baptist

Southeast

Lithonia

New Birth Missionary Baptist

Southwest

Fayetteville

Dogwood Church
ReGen Fellowship

Villa Rica

Midway Macedonia Baptist Church

Ministry Partners

And now for the orchestra, the ministry partners all over Atlanta. To be clear, these ministries are not partners with Unite! They are partners with the individual local churches of Unite! The list is not even close to exhaustive but rather a sampling. The ministry partners are arranged here according to the four strategic impact areas of poverty, education, justice, and family.

Poverty

Angel Food Ministries
Cobb Faith Partnership
Cut Out Hunger Charity Tables
Duluth Cooperative Ministry
Feed the Hungry Foundation
Fuller Center for Housing
Habitat for Humanity
Home Repairs Ministries
Lawrenceville Cooperative Ministry
Lilburn Cooperative Ministry
Movers and Shakers
No One Hungry

Norcross Cooperative Ministry
North Fulton Community Charities
North Gwinnett Cooperative Ministry

Health Care

Foundation for Hospital Art
Good Samaritan Health Center of Cobb
Good Samaritan Health Center of Fulton
Good Samaritan Health Center of Gwinnett

Homelessness

Atlanta Community Ministries

Atlanta Day Shelter
Family Promise of Gwinnett County, Inc.
Gwinnett Coalition Taskforce for the
Homeless
Mary Hall Freedom House
Trinity Life Church—Meals for the
Homeless

Education

The Bible Class
Core Foundations (Christian Learning
Centers)
Norcross Christian Learning Center
Turn Around Coaching
Unite! Directory of Public School Liaisons

Justice

Abuse and Exploitation

Awake Ministries
Innocence Atlanta
National Coalition for the Protection of
Children and Families
Sisters in Service

Elderly and Disabled

Annandale Village
Delmar Gardens
Embracing Hospice
Hi-Hope Center for Mentally Disabled
Ivy Hall Assisted Living
Lilburn Health and Rehabilitation Center
Meadowbrook Nursing Home
Metro Atlanta Recovery Residence
Peachtree Christian Hospice
Plantation South Assisted Living
Sunrise Assisted Living

Family

Autism Society of America—Greater
Georgia Chapter
Georgia Family Council
Single Parent 411
SPECTRUM Autism Support Group
Camps and Clubs

Adoption/Crisis Pregnancy

Beacon of Hope
Bethany Christian Services
Foster Care Support Foundation, Inc.
Foster Children's Foundation
Gwinnett Pregnancy Resource Center
promise686

Apartment Ministries

Flood Student Missions
Me and My House
Whirlwind Missions
Youth Outreach United

Children's Shelters

Atlanta Children's Shelter
Children's Restoration Network
Gwinnett Children's Shelter
Jesse's House

Drug and Alcohol Rehabilitation

Barnabas Ministries
Good Samaritan Ministries
Purple, Inc.

Internationals and Refugees

Amigos for Christ
Refugee Resettlement and Immigration of
Atlanta
World Relief

Transitional Housing for Women and Children

House of Hope
Rainbow Village
Wellspring of Living Water Home

Youth at Risk

Boys and Girls Club of Lawrenceville
Christian Association of Youth Mentoring
Compass Ministries
The Crossings Ranch
Cross Walk Ministries

Eagle Ranch
Gwinnett Youth Detention Center
Ministry
I Am BEAUTIFUL, Inc.

Metro Atlanta Youth for Christ
Street GRACE
YMCA Lawrenceville

And the Song Never Ends

A book like this is difficult to end. Not because there is more to write about vision or strategy or planning. It's hard to end because the stories don't. The combined movement of the churches of Unite! has produced story upon story of God's transforming power. In addition, the stories of friendships continue to develop and deepen as we sing together. The stories spring from those places where the choir and the orchestra intersect. Not long ago, a volunteer from one of our Unite! churches attended an event at one of our partner ministries and observed this intersection firsthand:

> Rainbow Village, a shelter for families in our area, and some of our partner churches recently gathered for a graduation ceremony. A young man spoke briefly of a life lived in dingy hotels and cars. When he was in the sixth grade, he and his mother moved into Rainbow Village and began to sing a new song. "I came to Rainbow Village when I was twelve years old," he said. "And for the first time in my life I attended the same school all year long. I made friends, I had stability. And I watched my mother change, and I became so proud of her."
>
> The young man took his seat and glanced at his mother, now the Children and Youth Program Director at Rainbow Village. She smiled at him and reached to gently cup his face in her hands, offering her own pride back to him as a gift.[1]

As soon as the last word is written here, another life or school or family or neighborhood will begin to sing and dance to God's tune. Somewhere in our city, the song will erupt anew and, when the music starts, so will the miracle of transformation. That's because our God is big—big enough to meet the needs all around us and big enough to use us to do it, no matter how small we are.

Don't tell small it can't do big.

GMC ad online

Bless the small, bless the great.

    Psalm 115:13 Message

The whole earth falls to its knees—it worships you, sings to you, can't stop enjoying your name and fame.

    Psalm 66:4 Message

Appendix 1

Community Outreach

How Perimeter Church Developed Its Community Outreach Department (2002)

It is important to note that prayer is the foundation on which this ministry was built. Each step in our formation process was and will be undergirded by prayer. We include prayer in our decision-making process. Each church staff member and lay leader has individual prayer partners who focus on praying specifically for each person in leadership.

1. Mercy Ministry Task Force—A committee was formed in September 2001 to begin praying about the direction God was leading our church in pursuing his heart of mercy ministry to the community around us. The committee (and church) hired a ministry consultant to help put together a strategic plan for a mercy focus for Perimeter Church. The committee's recommendation was to create a new department with a focus on mobilizing the church to meet needs in the community. Thus, the Perimeter Community Outreach department was formed.

2. Hiring of staff—In the summer of 2002, Perimeter Church hired three full-time Community Outreach staff persons: a director, an associate, and an administrative assistant.
3. Defining our geographic ministry focus—We decided to focus on a twelve-mile radius of the church in order to allow our members the opportunity to serve in locations that are no more than a thirty-minute drive from their homes. In addition, we found substantial needs even in suburban Atlanta.
4. Demographic research—Once we defined our target area, we wanted to find out what the needs really were in our community. We hired two seminary students for eight weeks during the summer of 2002 to research the twelve-mile radius. They conducted demographic research as well as many interviews with individuals, groups, and organizations in the community to find out the needs and who was already meeting those needs.
5. Defining our areas of serving—As a result of our research, we decided to focus on four people groups (or areas of need).
   - internationals—immigrants and refugees
   - women and family—focus on single moms and their children and women in crisis
   - youth—at-risk children and teens
   - dependents—elderly and disabled
6. Developing partnerships—Instead of trying to create a new ministry on our own, we decided to partner with existing ministries and organizations. We focus on two types of partnerships:
   - ministries and organizations—We are forming partnerships with ministries and organizations that are already doing a great job of addressing and meeting needs in the community.
   - other churches—We firmly believe that if we want to see our community brought to life in a transforming encounter with the kingdom of God, then churches must unite and partner together to meet needs in the community.
7. Community team structure—As opposed to serving as individuals, we chose to build our mercy ministry foundation on the idea of serving together as teams. We believe the team structure will enable our people to receive shepherding, training, and

guidance as they serve. The purpose of the community team is fourfold: (1) to serve as the "champion" for the partner, (2) to identify the needs of the partner, (3) to communicate the needs to the church, and (4) to help mobilize the church to serve the people in need through the partner. We look at the community team as the bridge between the church and the community (partner).

8. Lay leadership development—We believe strongly in developing a deep lay leadership structure to provide much of the ministry oversight. We have lay directors for each of the four areas (internationals, women and family, youth, and dependants) and community team leaders who are empowered, trained, and encouraged. We've also put together a Community Outreach Ministry Team (similar to an active board of directors) that provides oversight to the ministry. Our COMT includes twelve people: community outreach staff, lay area directors, a deacon liaison, a prayer coordinator, and a church networking representative.

9. Lay leadership training—We have developed a seven-week "mercy and compassion" training for area directors and community team leaders, as well as others with a heart for mercy. Area directors meet with community team leaders once per month for ongoing shepherding, training, and prayer.

10. Congregational opportunity for mercy "exposure"—In November 2002, we coordinated a full weekend of mercy outreach for our entire congregation. During our Compassion in Action Weekend, we coordinated about twenty mercy opportunities for people to experience. The goal was not only to give people an opportunity to serve but more importantly to give them a "taste" of mercy ministry. We have found that an "exposure" to the needs and a "taste" of mercy are key factors in bringing to life God's heart of mercy in the lives of our people.

Appendix 2

Unite!

Creating an Ongoing Movement

1. Pray, Pray, Pray

The most important thing we did was pray for God to unite his body in our area. We have made this one of our primary strategies for all churches that work together on an ongoing basis.

2. Cast a Vision

It is critically important that your church identify with and grasp the importance of:

- being externally focused by serving in your community.
- developing partnerships with other churches, ministries, and organizations. Unite! is based on churches serving and blessing the community together, which includes defining emphasis areas and/or partners in the community, raising up lay leadership, and determining a plan to mobilize the church.

3. Build Relationships

To be successful at developing partnerships between churches, it is of primary importance to build relationships among staff and lay leaders in the churches. For example, friendships were developed in Atlanta at monthly area pastors' gatherings. A couple of churches initiated lunch gatherings specifically for community outreach or local missions staff, which helped build relationships that have led to friendships.

4. Invite Others

The beginnings of Unite! can be traced to a pastors' luncheon in which Perimeter Church simply invited Hopewell Missionary Baptist to join hands to serve the community. Most churches that get involved do so because they were personally asked. It really can begin with just two churches.

5. Define the Project or Effort

Unite! was developed using Fellowship Bible Church's Sharefest (www.sharefest.org) as a model. Using Matthew 5:16 as our guide, churches in Atlanta decided to define our effort as "praying, serving, and celebrating together" for the purpose of community transformation. In October of 2003, a weekend of serving and blessing the community was formed (Compassion in Action) followed by a Heaven on Earth celebration the following Sunday evening at a local arena.

6. Provide Leadership

In addition to identifying an overall leader, or director, to give leadership to Unite!, an overall leadership team made up of representatives from eight churches was formed. This team is very diverse ethnically, culturally, and denominationally. In addition, planning teams were developed for Compassion in Action and for the Heaven on Earth celebration.

7. Provide a Statement of Faith

Relationships are easiest to establish and develop when we first focus on our similarities instead of our differences. We do, however, need to agree on the basic essentials of the Christian faith. A statement of faith helps to determine what beliefs are most important and nonnegotiable. Unite! adopted the Lausanne Covenant, which is a broadly evangelical document balancing word and deed ministry.

8. Communicate

One of the greatest challenges of bridging the gaps between churches is developing an effective means of clear communication. Possibilities include postcards, letters, brochures, websites, emails, etc. All are good, but the best form of communication is a phone call or personal visit. In addition, a monthly luncheon provides a great forum for communicating, building relationships, and inviting other churches to join the common effort. The main purpose of a luncheon would be to cast vision, build relationships, plan, and pray for the community and one another. A luncheon can be held at a local cafeteria, allowing everyone to pay for their own meals and receive their food in a timely manner.

9. Provide Long-term Planning

From the start, Unite! leadership decided that if we were going to see transformation occur within our community, our efforts would need to be ongoing. We could not just come together annually to serve during a big event.

Long-term planning includes the following:

- The leadership team members develop vision and mission statements.
- They meet monthly to plan, continue along the overall vision, and chart progress.
- They develop a central means of distributing communications (i.e., a website; see www.UniteUs.org).
- They host monthly luncheons for the purpose of casting vision, networking, and sharing about needs in the community.
- They host gatherings of community outreach lay leaders from the churches to talk about how to serve together in the community.

Appendix 3

A Study of Duluth

Project Overview

Partnership
Duluth churches worked together on a twelve-month research project to help us understand the history, culture, spiritual climate, areas of need, and opportunities for transformation in Duluth. Churches committed to this research project, initially, were Perimeter Church, Duluth First Baptist, Friendship Baptist Church, Duluth UMC, Sugarloaf UMC, and Korean Church of Atlanta.

Basic Premise
The basic premise behind this in-depth study of Duluth was the belief that "the more we know about the history of Duluth, the more we will care about its future." It was our desire, as churches, to discover where God had been at work in Duluth, what he was doing now, and how we could be used by God to transform Duluth for his great glory.

Two Primary Objectives
The two primary objectives we hoped to achieve were: (1) a comprehensive guidebook from a biblical and holistic perspective on

Duluth's past, present, and future; and (2) new collaborative relationships that would lend themselves to helping churches impact and bless Duluth.

Three Phases
Phase 1 (January–June): Research and Interviews

Duluth churches invited volunteers to be a part of one of three volunteer teams (three to ten people per team) that would (1) build a database of influential people in Duluth to interview; (2) compile research about Duluth from websites, writings, and books; and (c) interview influential people in Duluth about Duluth.

A pastors' learning community was established for the purpose of laying a biblical foundation for transformation. The pastors also discussed the findings as the project was taking place. This community met for an hour once per month for twelve months.

Volunteer Opportunities (one to three hours per week, through June)

- database development team (three to five volunteers): developed a database of people in Duluth for the purpose of conversations that would yield information about Duluth's history, culture, government, social hurts and ills, needs, and opportunities
- research team (five to ten volunteers): gathered information about Duluth from websites, books, historical documents, and public records
- conversation team (five to ten volunteers): gathered information about Duluth by talking with people (as identified by the database development team)

Phase 2 (June–September): Focus Groups and Surveys

Focus groups were formed made up of leaders in education, business, media, arts and entertainment, government, and nonprofits. The focus groups discussed the major challenges that they saw in Duluth and in their channel and also the things that were making a positive difference. It was a forum to address the strengths and weaknesses and how we could all work together. Also, churches completed surveys that gave information on their congregation and what they were doing in their church and in the community.

Phase 3 (October–January): Writing and Data Analysis

Drue (Perimeter staff) and Travis compiled the information gathered in phases 1 and 2 and organized it into a comprehensive guidebook, primarily for Duluth churches.

Appendix 4

Community Research

A Relational, Asset-Based Approach

A community study with the goal of transformation does not mean academic analysis or armchair observations. We approach the community more like getting to know a friend than like studying a subject for a school report. This kind of study values building relationships with and seeking input from members of the community. It's fairly easy to find statistics on a community. Taking the time to be inclusive and relational will allow you to get beyond raw data to the heart of the matter. Forming relationships for the long haul also discourages the temptation to look for a quick fix for entrenched problems.

Think of your community study as a treasure hunt for the wheat of God's gifts and activity often hidden among the tares (Matt. 13:24–30). Begin by asking the Lord of the harvest to show you where his reign is already evident. A need-based paradigm—defining a community primarily in terms of needs and problems—can become demoralizing. It can lead to a patronizing attitude that perpetuates dependency by rescuing people rather than empowering them.

In contrast, an *asset-based* approach embraces four main principles:

1. God is already at work in the community. There is no place on earth that God has abandoned, that is excluded from God's loving presence and redemptive plan. God's work is not limited by funding, education, or abilities. God can use people who do not claim faith and institutions such as schools and businesses as instruments for good.
2. We are defined not by our problems but by our potential. Each person is precious, uniquely created in God's image. Each person has God-given gifts to offer and capacities to develop. Those we serve have more to offer back to us and to their community than we can imagine. The goal of ministry is not only to meet people's needs but also to release individuals to share their gifts with others.
3. Do ministry *with* people, not *to* people. The vision and plans for serving a community need to engage the input of people in the community. True development means empowering individuals and communities to achieve their own goals. Bringing people's dreams to light provides energy to work toward change.
4. Effective ministry builds on assets. Our first question is not What is wrong? but Where is God at work? We seek to get on board with the gifts and initiatives in the community that reflect what God is already doing. Beyond simply doing things for people, the church has a valuable role in coming alongside a community to help build people's capacity and unleash their potential.

A relational, asset-based approach nurtures relationships that connect members of the community to God and one another. This approach, writes Jay Van Groningen in *Communities First: Through God's Eyes, with God's Heart*, leads to "seeing all things in a community that can be used in some way to make life better for everyone" and "connecting people in wonderful exchanges of neighborly love." This paradigm helps a church move from analysis to action.[1]

Notes

Chapter 1: A New Kind of Big

1. www.colormatters.com/colortheory.html.

Chapter 2: Turning Our Hearts Inside Out

1. www.nmsa.org/Publications/MiddleSchoolJournal/September2002/Article10/tabid/418/Default.aspx.

2. http://my.safaribooksonline.com/9780596517717/the_value_of_writing_things_ down.

3. Randy Pope, *The Intentional Church: Moving from Church Success to Community Transformation* (Chicago: Moody, 2006).

4. For more information on our second research project, see appendix 3 and http://pingu.salk.edu/~sefton/Hyper_protocols/growcells.html.

5. Ibid.

Chapter 3: Big Questions with Big Answers

1. Bill Osinski, "Katrina Aftermath: Lains Find Comfort in New Family, Long Term Needs Being Met," *Atlanta Journal-Constitution*, October 23, 2005, JJ1.

2. For a more comprehensive time line of these events, see appendix 1.

3. Robert Lewis, *The Church of Irresistible Influence* (Grand Rapids: Zondervan, 2001).

4. http://copgny.org/230709.ihtml.

5. http://nycleadership.com/default.aspx.

6. www.rcpc.com/page.jsp?navigation=14.

Chapter 4: Diagram of a Dream

1. www.lausanne.org.

2. www.wellspringliving.org.

3. See appendix 3.

4. http://web.mit.edu/invent/iow/altschul.html.

5. www.jdpower.com/corporate/news/releases/pdf/2007219.pdf.

6. http://knowledge.wpcarey.asu.edu/article.cfm?articleid=1616.

7. www.evangelismcoach.org/2009/statistics-on-invitations-to-church.

Chapter 5: The Epic Becomes Us

1. Ben Ortlip, *The End of the Spear: The Beginning of the Lesson* (Nashville: Thomas Nelson, 2006), 96.

2. David Pinault, *Story-Telling Techniques in The Arabian Nights* (Leiden, The Netherlands: E. J. Brill, 1992), 18.

Chapter 6: The Human Chain

1. http://query.nytimes.com/gst/abstract.html?res=9C00EFD7173EE733A257 55C2A9649D946797D6CF.

2. www.gwinnettdailypost.com/main.asp?Search=1&ArticleID=62601&Secti onID=6&SubSectionID=&S=1.

3. www.hihopecenter.org.

4. www.insidegwinnett.com/index2.php.

5. http://video.forbes.com/fvn/lifestyle/mk_sopranos060807_jal.

6. www.medievaltymes.com/courtyard/chainmaille_history.htm.

7. www.presstelegram.com/poverty.

8. www.hflb.org/about_hope_for_long_beach.html.

9. Thyda Duang, "New Hope, New Normal," *Long Beach Business Journal*, October 14, 2008.

10. Ibid.

Chapter 7: Transformation

1. Notes for this training material and any current material may be found at www.perimeter.org/communityoutreach.

2. Tim Keller, *Ministries of Mercy: The Call of the Jericho Road* (Phillipsburg, NJ: P & R Publishing, 1997).

3. Taken from http://touchedbyservice.blogspot.com (along with a shout-out to Greg Lang. Thanks, Greg!).

4. Ibid.

5. Ibid.

6. www.nehemiah-group.org.

7. www.missionhouston.org/Mission_Houston/MHUs.html.

Chapter 8: Unity

1. "The Status of Christianity and Religions in the Modern World," in *World Christian Encyclopedia*, 2nd ed., vol. 1, ed. David B. Barrett, George Thomas Kurian, and Todd M. Johnson (New York: Oxford University Press, 2001), 3.

2. Eric Swanson and Sam Williams, *To Transform a City* (Grand Rapids: Zondervan, 2010), 137.

3. Jack B. Rogers and Robert E. Blade, "The Great Ends of the Church: Two Perspectives," *Journal of Presbyterian History* 76 (1998): 181–86.

4. www.abpnews.com/index.php?option=com_content&task=view&id=4077&Itemid=61.

5. http://library.thinkquest.org/17940/texts/atom/atom.html.

6. http://library.thinkquest.org/17940/texts/fission/fission.html.

7. www.aip.org/history/mod/fission/fission1/01.html.

Chapter 9: We Have Liftoff

1. http://history.nasa.gov/SP-4110/vol2.pdf.

2. www.channel4.com/science/microsites/E/equinox/rocket_science.html#c4navSki.

3. www.christianitytoday.com/le/2007/summer/7.81.html.

4. Rick Badie, "A Love That Bridges Barriers," *Atlanta Journal-Constitution*, October 13, 2003, A1.

5. www.valuebasedmanagement.net/methods_rogers_innovation_adoption_curve.html.

6. The current edition of this guide may be purchased from Compassion Coalition at www.compassioncoalition.org.

7. Regarding children in single-parent households: U.S. Census Bureau, American Community Study, Knox County, 2005–2007 average annual estimates. Regarding homelessness and children: email correspondence with Dr. Roger Nooe, author of "Homelessness in Knoxville/Knox County 2008" (East Tennessee Coalition to End Homelessness). Regarding infant mortality among both black and white infants: Tennessee Department of Health Vital Statistics (2007 data), http://health.state.tn.us/statistics/vital.htm. Regarding abuse of children in Knox County: "Kids Count: The State of the Child 2007" (Tennessee Commission on Children and Youth, 2008).

8. Data from www.Guidestar.com and "Volunteering in America," Corporation for National and Community Service (www.volunteeringinamerica.gov), 2005–2008 annual average.

9. *Salt and Light: A Guide to Loving Knoxville*, 3rd ed. (Compassion Coalition, 2009), 349.

10. Ibid., 298.

11. Andy Rittenhouse, introduction to ibid., viii.

Chapter 10: Orbit

1. www.nasa.gov/mission_pages/shuttle/shuttlemissions/sts128/main/index.html.
2. Landa Cope, *The Old Testament Template: Rediscovering God's Principles for Discipling All Nations* (Cape Town, South Africa: Template Institute Press, 2007).
3. www.qideas.org/essays/influencing-culture.aspx.
4. Ibid.
5. www.smallgroups.com/articles/2009/missionalrenaissance.html.
6. www.cnn.com/2009/CRIME/10/26/child.prostitution.
7. Bill Osinski, "Churches Plan to Lend Hand in Public Schools," *Atlanta Journal-Constitution*, August 13, 2005, JJ3.

Chapter 11: Measuring Success

1. http://missionhouston-transformation.blogspot.com/2008_05_01_archive.html.
2. Ibid.
3. See appendix 3.
4. www.juvenilejusticefund.org/documents/Dear%20John%20Campaign%20Launch.pdf.

Chapter 12: Making Music

1. www.touchedbyservice.blogspot.com.

Appendix 4

1. This information is taken from Heidi Unruh, *Community Study Guide: Connect with Your Church's Context for Ministry*. To read a fuller treatment of the topic, look at the "Community Study Guide and Tools" in the resources section of Compassion Coalition's website: www.compassioncoalition.org. For more help on an asset-based approach to community study, see the resources available on the website for the Communities First Association (www.communitiesfirstassociation.org).

Chip Sweney is the Next Gen and Community Transformation Pastor and on the Executive Leadership Team at Perimeter Church in Johns Creek, Georgia. He oversees the ministry that Perimeter is doing outside the four walls of the church in metro Atlanta as well as all the partnering that Perimeter is doing with churches around metro Atlanta. He has been on staff at Perimeter for fourteen years and was one of the student ministry pastors before helping launch Community Outreach at Perimeter in 2002.

Chip also serves as the director of Unite!, a network of over 150 churches in Atlanta that are working together to see kingdom transformation in this city. Unite! was launched in 2003 in northeast Atlanta and is now spreading all over the metro area. Chip was one of the founders and serves on the board for Street GRACE, an alliance of churches in Atlanta that are working together with the public and private sector to bring the commercial sexual exploitation of children to an end in Atlanta.

Chip graduated from Duke University and received his MDiv from Trinity Evangelical Divinity School. He is ordained in the PCA denomination.

Chip has been married to his wonderful wife, Leigh Ann, for twenty years, and they have two children—Caroline, who is fourteen years old, and Jack, who is twelve.

Kitti Murray is a wife, mother, mother-in-law, and grandmother. She and her husband, Bill, live in downtown Atlanta, where they are part of a network of urban church planters. Kitti graduated from Agnes Scott College in 1978 with a degree in English/creative writing and German.

a ministry of perimeter church

Gospel-Centered Transformation

Recent studies have revealed that spiritual growth is a significant challen
facing today's church. Two side effects of this deficit of mature and equipp
followers of Christ are:

1) Church members satisfied with internal church program
   offerings for them; and
2) Churches becoming strong in external efforts through deed
   but not seeing much Kingdom growth as the harvesters
   struggle in presenting the Word.

Transforming a family, city, or the world for Christ relies on two critical el
ments: a mature believer equipped to share the gospel and a church that
intentional about being externally focused and open to collaborating wi
other like-minded churches.

Life on Life Ministries offers a way to invest in both of these
transformational elements. It provides resources for spiritual developme
through life-on-life missional discipleship.

For complete information, contact:
678.405.2238
www.lifeonlife.org

Metro Outreach Ministries assists churches in becoming externally focus
and networked with other community churches.

For complete information, contact:
678.405.2164
www.perimeter.org/metrooutreach

Perimeter
CHURCH